Jobless Diaries

Tips and Consolations for the Unemployed

978-1-326-95677-6
Imprint: Lulu.com

Copyright © 2024 Joni Putkinen

All rights reserved.

CONTENTS

Preface 1

PART 1

1   A few thoughts about being unemployed 6
2   Let's talk about money 9
3   Save money, no matter what 12
4   Wise spending 14
5   What will take you out of your rut? 17
6   Individuality getting hammered by social pressures 22
7   Self-confidence 25
8   Balanced unemployment 28
9   The unemployed hustle 30
10   Act before you're ready 33
11   Intermediate level 37
12   The unemployed businessman 39
13   Mission statement 42
14   Were you raised by an employee or an entrepreneur? 45
15   Waiting for retirement 49
16   The job interview mindset 54
17   It's up to the employer to decide who to employ 56

18	Downside, downside in my mind	58
19	Best for you is not best for me	60
20	Who is responsible for unemployment?	69
21	Luck is always involved in business and life	72

PART 2

Increase your chances for success 77

1 Write down your goals 77

2 Define your strategy and parameters for failure and success, then stick to that strategy and only change it when absolutely necessary 79

3 Make a concrete plan of how you are going to make money in near future 80

4 Use the method of approximating expected value 82

5 Never evaluate your actions 'after the fact' 84

6 Maximize your options 85

7 Learn from experience and refine your approach 87

8 Light a fire under your ass, the right way 89

9 Be careful with comparisons 90

10 Read to increase your optionality 92

11 Protect yourself from downside 93

12 Be patient 95

13 Get ready to disappoint others 96

Epilogue 99

About the author 101

Literature / suggested readings 103

Preface

These diaries were written during the evenings of my unemployment. They blend rational contemplation, analyses of unemployment in general and consolations for those struggling with similar feelings and emotions. These reflections helped me stay sane and sensible during my own unemployment journey.

In this book I explore how society and others can drive us to do irrational things when we're unemployed — things that don't help us achieve what we need to do. Some of these issues are difficult to discuss with family or friends, who might not fully understand even if we tried to explain.

It often feels like the world is moving forward while you're stuck at home, grappling with the disappointment of repeated rejections. Each glimmer of hope seems quickly dashed, leaving you to wonder: Why am I not getting noticed or even responded to?

There's also the persistent fear: Will I ever find a job? How can I move past this phase and become a productive employee again? Am I setting unrealistic expectations for myself? These are common fears that haunt the unemployed, making unemployment one of the most taxing phases of life.

Unemployment comes with its own set of taboos, topics that are difficult to talk about. Personally I've found some comfort in watching other jobless individuals share their experiences on YouTube and other forums. However, many of these videos focus on lifestyle tips, budgets and superficial advice on job searching, which may not delve deeply into the emotional pain of unemployment.

This is why I decided to write these diaries. I believe there is a need for a book that addresses common experiences and problems associated with unemployment, offering a reflective but compassionate look that readers can digest privately, at their own pace. I am not a career coach and cannot offer specific advice on landing your dream job. Instead I share my personal experiences and reflections, combining what I've thought, seen and read.

I have also faced moments of feeling lost and overwhelmed by the uncertainty of unemployment. My strength lies in my ability to think clearly under distress, though emotion cannot always be overcome by reason alone. I use reason to guide myself toward a path where I can balance my passions and feelings.

I'm not here to give advice on polishing your résumé or assigning blame. Each person must decide what is rational for their own situation. What works for me might not work for you.

Nevertheless, I want to offer you something useful. In part two of this book I offer 13 actionable tips and exercises that can improve your job search and overall life. These tips are effective for anyone regardless of their employment status — whether unemployed, employed, an entrepreneur or retired.

Despite cultural differences in how work is perceived, we share the same human condition with similar needs and challenges. We can understand each other's goals and feelings even when we disagree on the best approaches.

If you're reading this while unemployed, know that there is hope. Unemployment is a tough battle with more disappointments than successes. Overcoming this requires using your head and taking care of yourself before expecting positive outcomes.

For that purpose, I offer well-thought-out snippets of advice for the reader to reflect on, with the hope that they will consider how to integrate them into their own life – whether they are unemployed, trying to understand the unemployed or preparing for the inevitable bouts of unemployment that many of us will face more than once in our lifetime.

In addition to being useful for the unemployed, I believe this book can also help those who want to better understand these issues or who seek to empathize with how the unemployed feel and think. It encourages all of us to step outside the framework of work and employment contracts for a moment and reflect on what truly matters to each of us. It invites us to consider how we can use money to pursue our personal endeavors and dreams, rather than letting money control our lives.

This book is divided into two parts. The first part, 'Consolations,' consists of essays that explore unemployment and work life from various perspectives. The second part, 'Tips,' provides actionable advice with commentary and instructions. I recommend starting with the essays, as reading them first will help you better understand the tips and the philosophy behind them. However, each essay and tip is designed to be comprehensible on its own.

At the end of the book, I've included a short list of recommended readings. Each of these books has had a significant impact on the way I think about work and employment. I'm confident you won't be disappointed once you explore them.

PART 1

1   A few thoughts about being unemployed

Nobody enjoys being unemployed if the goal is to have a job, and we generally assume that having a job is more socially acceptable than not having one. Without the pressure of social comparison, unemployment can actually be quite satisfying and even a source of great joy.

What I hate most about being unemployed is that people who aren't unemployed often think they know how I should spend my time and where I should apply. They'd be willing to take the first job they can get just to be done with it. Yet, if I manage to land a great job after months of effort and keeping my expectations high, they rationalize it by saying they always knew I was capable and deserving of such a position.

You really shouldn't take advice from others (unless they have something to lose themselves), because they don't know your goals, they don't think the way you do and they have nothing to gain. Always remember that.

But for me, everything is clear. I know what I need to do. I've got my act together. I have a strategy and I have a backup plan in case my strategy fails. Everything is in perfect order. And even if that order breaks, I can easily adapt and readjust. It doesn't matter how my actions appear to others — they're on the outside, trying to look in and understand.

I've seen countless times how to outsiders it seems like I'd be better off doing meaningless tasks all day, just so I could report to my friends and family that I've been 'active'. But I'd rather focus on maximizing the rationality of my actions and concentrating on the things that increase my chances of getting what I want through the strategy I've chosen.

An unemployed person makes an asymmetric bet every time they apply for a job. This is a fact that somehow escapes most people. You only need to win once — that's the name of the game. We all play with probabilities in life, whether we acknowledge it or not. When someone makes an asymmetric bet, it means the potential reward is great, even though the chances of success might be slim. But the expected reward can still make it worthwhile. It's entirely rational to stick with a strategy that fails most of the time if the potential payoff is high. When sending out job applications, you're likely to fail far more often than succeed, probably with a terrible win-to-fail ratio. So why not make the most of each bet?

Nobody knows the true odds of the job market, which only adds to the rationality of sticking with a strategy 'until the pockets are empty' — in other words, only abandoning the strategy when you absolutely must and lowering your expectations at that point. Until then, it's completely rational and justified to stick with the chosen plan.

When I make asymmetric bets, I ensure there's minimal downside and maximum upside. When I apply for a job, I make sure it's a good fit for me and meets my expectations. I have little to lose and a lot to gain, so why not aim higher than what I think I'm currently capable of based on my work experience and skills? I also apply to more positions than I think are necessary, because doing so increases my chances and creates opportunities for unexpected successes.

Of course, there's the risk that I might end up in a job I hate, one that could destroy my well-being. There's also the risk of losing money while waiting for those golden opportunities to appear. But I believe that risk is smaller compared to the long-term damage of working in a job that ruins your life. You can always find ways to make and save money in the future, but staying too long in a toxic work environment can have far-reaching negative effects that can lead to a downward spiral.

And what about the upside? Well, there's far more variation in the outcomes of good fortune. You might get a decent job with decent pay or you could land a fantastic job with fantastic pay. In the game of job hunting, there are always more losers than winners, but every applicant hopes to win at least once in this winner-takes-all scenario.

The asymmetry becomes most apparent when you aim for greater rewards. Some prefer a safer approach with lower risk and lower returns. You'll find these people in every workplace, complaining about their jobs, saying they'd rather be elsewhere or that they wouldn't work if they had enough money (though they've never really tried to save). They never take that crucial step where they can say: 'I've tested the limits of my capabilities and luck. I've done everything I can, and now I can accept my place in this world'.

Thinking about employment and unemployment requires a sense of optionality that many lack. When you have money, you can approach work more rationally. You begin to realize that money is the most important factor. You can trade money for freedom and use that freedom to pursue more money. This is the ultimate trade-off between work and wealth. When you have the option not to work, you can reject the silliness of social norms and make money in ways that suit you best. It doesn't have to be a traditional 9-to-5 job. It could be something completely different.

Once you're in a position where you can save money and have savings, you can finally start thinking about work in terms of money. You begin calculating how long your savings can sustain you without a job and you start weighing the time spent working against both its monetary and emotional value. The more you focus on the monetary value of work, the less appealing it becomes. It's no longer the obvious choice it once was. You start thinking, 'I'm not valuing myself enough. I'm selling myself short and sacrificing what truly matters for the sake of paid labor instead of focusing on my own happiness. I'm making a trade-off that I shouldn't be making'.

2   Let's talk about money

Let's talk about money more concretely, then. I do paid labor only under two conditions. The first is that I work to sustain myself when I'm broke. The second is that I work to save money when I'm not. If I'm not able to save money while working, then I would find myself in a regrettable and sad situation. There are millions of people who are not able to save after necessary expenses. I would rather be poor and save at least something than be rich, save nothing and be ridden with problems that come with an expensive lifestyle.

What about income? What kind of income should you aim for? That's a type of decision that's for each person to decide for themselves, but let me give an example that might put salary strategizing in a clearer perspective.

Suppose you're unemployed with three options: 1) accept a job offering 2350 € per month[1], 2) wait for a potentially better-paying job or 3) remain unemployed and rely on unemployment benefits or social welfare. What would you do?

The decision depends on various factors, some more significant than others. In some cases it might be better to stay on unemployment benefits if the economic incentives to work aren't favorable. If working would result in lower net income than your benefits, staying home might be rational. However, I won't delve into the other benefits of work here as I don't believe in exchanging money for work just for the sake of working. While some, like my parents with a Protestant work ethic, might disagree, their criteria may not be money-focused.

Despite this I encourage seeking employment as the benefits of work are not accessible without actively pursuing it. It's beneficial to seek well-paid jobs even if you don't need one right away.

---

[1] As for reference, in Finland you can easily live with that kind money but not save much, especially if you live in an urban area and have family to take care of.

Taking the first job offered might not be the best strategy. If you accept a €2350-per-month job immediately, you miss the potential for higher earnings and saving more money. Patience can be rewarded; waiting a year without income to secure a €3200-per-month job could put you in a better financial position in the long run. For instance, after working 3.83 years at €3200 per month, you'd be in the same financial position as if you'd taken the €2350 job immediately.[2] With a €4000-per-month salary, the financial advantage of waiting comes even sooner.

The assumptions here are reasonable. If you can secure a €2350 job easily, there are likely opportunities for better-paying positions. Many employers offer only the minimum salary for a role. If €2350 is the minimum, some employers might offer €2650 or more. Positions with greater responsibility and higher pay are also worth exploring. Applying for such roles allows you to gauge and potentially increase your market value, directing your efforts more effectively.

Emotionally it may be challenging to adopt a purely rational strategy, but financially it could be advantageous. This approach sets you up for future success, enhances your self-worth and provides a year of financial flexibility without

---

[2] This calculation is based on taxes that prevail in the state of Finland at the time of writing and different tax brackets are included. Also in Finland you wouldn't have to be without money for a year unless you really wanted that.

significant long-term negative effects. Additionally, you'd receive higher unemployment benefits if you lose your job.

I believe that unemployment or being without an employment contract sometimes offers a clearer perspective on money. When you're not trading time for money, you can better understand what money means to you personally without the distortions of employment demands. Being broke can be more dangerous than being unemployed.

3 Save money, no matter what

For some making money comes easily, but it has never been that way for me. I've been completely broke for most of my life, so I understand what it means to be poor. My net worth has improved over the past few years; it was negative for a long time, and I carried over €15,000 in student debt.

The reason I'm now in a better financial position is not that I've become more skillful in earning money, wiser or a better investor.[3] I have become adept at saving money, but saving alone isn't enough to be wealthy. You also need to earn enough to save. I've worked for an employer for several years and saved as much as possible from my pay. I'm grateful that I was seen as bringing enough value to be employed, which

---

[3] Everyone likes to view themselves positively. I find it really painful when there's a significant gap between what I believe I'm capable of earning and what I'm actually earning. This discrepancy can make me feel less capable than I thought.

allowed me to eliminate my debt and save enough to finally rest without financial worries.

Today our self-worth is often tied to materialistic consumerism, a culture that glorifies those who can both earn and spend large amounts of money. Saving money is sometimes viewed as just another way to earn, as the saying goes, you "need to put money to work" and let it snowball. If you can't save money as effectively as the best investors, you might be seen as a failure. Haven't you noticed all those bank commercials promising riches if you only have the wisdom to invest wisely in stocks or well-managed funds?

Joblessness represents the risk of falling back into financial difficulty. I save money to reduce the risk of becoming poor and unhappy, not to "make it work," "outperform the market" or buy a house. You don't need a specific reason to save money. "Save, save, save," as Morgan Housel advises in his book *The Psychology of Money*.[4] There's little downside to having money in your bank account. While it might not be the most rational strategy, it's a reasonable one and helps me sleep peacefully at night.

Financial experts often recommend investing to protect against inflation. Theoretically they are justified in this claim. However, you should be concerned about inflation only when it's high, not when it's around two percent. Focus on

---

[4] Housel's *The Psychology of Money* (2020) is the best book anyone can read about money in my opinion; it's not technical or filled with expert literature and references, instead it contains a lot practical wisdom that gives you much to think about.

maintaining peace of mind and a reasonable financial strategy that keeps you independent and level-headed, even during times of high distress and personal trouble.

4 Wise spending

You never want your lavish lifestyle to limit your options, especially when you're unemployed. In Finland, for example, renting an apartment that costs €900 per month is impractical if you're unemployed, on social welfare or earning a minimum salary. The only way to afford comfortable and spacious living is through consistent income (or support from relatives). A substantial monthly expense can be a significant burden, potentially jeopardizing your entire household economy if something unexpected occurs.

Many people only realize this too late. In Finland our current government is cutting housing benefits substantially and reducing income-based daily allowances for the unemployed in multiple phases. Those who have relied on taxpayer-subsidized housing benefits and are now forced to move to cheaper apartments often find it challenging due to a lack of savings. Many have lived beyond their means, relying on the assumption that government support would continue indefinitely. I don't share that faith, which is why I live frugally even when receiving government assistance.

When faced with unemployment, my first step is to minimize overhead as much as possible. Even though I don't indulge in extravagant spending, unemployment provides a strong incentive to cut unnecessary expenses. Currently, the only subscription service I have is my wireless internet connection, costing €9.99 per month. I don't have Netflix or a mobile phone subscription (I use prepaid).

If you have multiple subscription services, calculate the annual cost. For example, Elisa's limitless mobile phone subscription with 10 Mbit/s speed costs €27.99 per month (+ €9.99 for the opening payment) as of September 2024 in Finland. The total for the first year would be €345.87. For me, that's a significant amount and I believe my money has better uses, so I choose not to invest in it.

I approach my finances as if I were running a startup with a limited budget. By spending frugally, I can extend my financial resources. I maintain an income statement and a balance sheet of my personal finances, updating them regularly to keep track of my income and expenses.

I buy non-perishables in bulk and wait for the best prices. I compare prices at different stores and review price histories. I don't need to find the absolute lowest price but set a target price within a tight range and buy when it's reached. This strategy helps avoid buyer's remorse, knowing I purchased at a good price. It's also effective to buy when you don't expect prices to drop much further. Producers and retailers need to maintain profit margins, so prices are more likely to rise than fall. Long-term, buying essential non-perishables when they're cheap is a sound strategy.

I'm not suggesting you should live like a hermit or forgo life's little pleasures. Ultimately it's your choice how to use your hard-earned or not-so-earned money. Coffee, for instance, is a small pleasure I enjoy, even though it may not be the cheapest option.

Don't be afraid to make personal investments. Investing some of your money in areas that can enhance your future or improve your options is worthwhile. For example, if you work with a computer, investing in powerful components and quality peripherals can make long work sessions more manageable.

Similarly, invest in practical software for your needs. If you're a graphic designer, invest in high-quality design software. If you're a trader, choose excellent trading software. If you make videos, proper production equipment and editing software are beneficial. However, be reasonable; you don't need to empty your wallet to get started.

The goal of personal investments is not that you can't start projects without them, but that by acquiring useful tools, you signal to yourself that you're committed to your path and building an identity related to your investments and environment. For example, I used to admire streamers and coders with multiple monitors. Once I acquired two monitors for coding, I saw that it was totally worth it. The increased utility made tasks like coding, video editing, multitasking and writing much easier.

Initially I wasn't using the new equipment to its full potential, which reminded me to utilize it more effectively. As a result I took on projects that benefited from having multiple monitors and gradually improved my skills. This experience taught me that having useful tools can strengthen your commitment to your goals and help you become better in various areas. Ensure that your investments align with the identity you want to develop and push yourself to live that reality.

5   What will take you out of your rut?

One key question every unemployed person must answer after the hundredth rejection isn't, *Why am I not getting job offers?* or *Is there something wrong with me*? Instead, it's *How can I get out of this rut?*

We all face ruts when unemployed, sometimes quite often. It's essential to know how to climb out because we can't afford to stay stuck for too long. The stakes are too high. The longer you remain in a rut, the harder it is to escape.

What do I mean by "rut"? It's a state where you feel stuck, depressed and unable to move forward. You're doing things you know aren't good for you — eating poorly, sleeping irregularly, neglecting exercise. You lose initiative, prioritization and confidence. Worse, you're not doing what's needed to regain that confidence and keep active.

Your body is tired from the previous struggles, trying to conserve energy. If you were on a winning streak, you'd feel energized and unstoppable. But instead, you've taken another hit and now even simple tasks seem daunting.

So, how do you get out? Start by creating a routine. Stick to a steady sleep schedule, get out of bed when you're not sleeping, eat regularly and healthily and keep your living space tidy. Take care of yourself as you would normally. Exercise at least a couple of times a week, ideally every other day.

When you start projects early in the morning, it almost feels like going to work. This creates a sense of accomplishment, even when things are working against you. If a job rejection comes, you can say, *"No biggie. I picked berries this morning, got a full bucket and now I'm cleaning them while reflecting on what went wrong with my interview. At least I've got my berries. This day wasn't wasted and I still have the energy for tomorrow".*

Talk to family and friends, but try to avoid deep dives into job-search frustrations. Instead, discuss hobbies and things you would have talked about when you were employed. Focusing too much on your job search can turn into reliving negative experiences or even heated discussions that leave you feeling worse.

Share positive updates, like new job applications or productive things you've done that day. If you don't have anything to show, focus on doing something useful so you can be proud the next day. Positive interactions and useful actions lift your mood and build self-worth.

One way to escape a rut is to be useful to yourself and others. Doing something that others appreciate can boost your mood and make you feel productive. If you can't focus on big tasks, tackle something you've been postponing. For me, that was writing a book and improving my coding skills. Completing these long-postponed goals felt as good as landing a job. Once they were done, they no longer caused mental strain.

You can also reflect on the positives of your current situation. Early in my unemployment, creative and positive writing helped me tremendously. Here's a list of positives I came up with:

- I get to make my own choices in line with my values.

- I can help my family.

- I have the chance to improve skills that I couldn't while working.

- No annoying bosses.

- I can explore new and interesting opportunities.

This exercise reframed unemployment as an interesting phase of life and a challenge, rather than something to fear. Many people leave their jobs willingly, preferring unemployment over staying in their roles. Perhaps they, too, saw the benefits and freedom that unemployment can offer.

Wallowing in negative emotions only prolongs the pain. Instead, acknowledge your efforts and the reality that you can't always control the outcome. Getting a job can be incredibly hard and rejection is not a reflection of your worth. Lady Fortune may not be kind right now, but adopting a Stoic mindset can help you accept that life's events are neutral — it's your interpretation that makes them good or bad.

When you're in a rut, you begin to build resistance in your mind[5] but a rut is more insidious than just a bit of mental pushback. It's a vicious cycle. Anyone who's been unemployed for a while knows how easy it is to start rationalizing and doubting the path they've chosen. Staying strong is difficult when self-doubt accumulates and over time this mental resistance becomes a formidable barrier to progress.

I don't need to remind myself of every failure or force myself into a positive mindset when I wake up and make my morning porridge. Sure, I've failed a few times, but more than 99 percent of the time, my porridge turns out perfectly fine. My job search, however, has the opposite success rate. More than 99 percent of my applications have ended in failure. It's no surprise that my mind has become conditioned to expect rejection. It's hard not to when failure becomes the norm.

So whenever I get rejected in my job search, I might start to rationalize: *"This job wasn't a good fit for me anyway"* or

---

[5] The same kind of Resistance that Steven Pressfield talks about in his book *Turning Pro* – it stops us from doing the work that needs to be done. Resistance takes place right before it's time to roll up one's sleeves and get into work.

"Well, it's their loss because they clearly can't see how fabulous I am". But that's bullshit and deep down I know it. It's healthier to admit, *"I wanted that job, I really did, but life is full of disappointments. I'd rather take this as a challenge than let myself get crushed by this small adversity. If I continue, I might get what I want and it will taste sweeter than any achievement before that"*.

You shouldn't let bad days deter you from following your path. We've all had those days. Today, as I'm writing this, I've been unemployed for almost three months. It's plenty of time to start doubting my strategy. I start to think: *"Is this the right approach for me?"*, *"How much longer can I keep doing this?"*, *"Why is life so hard for me and why am I not getting rewarded for all my effort?"*, *"Is this strategy working?"* and *"How much longer can I keep doing this?"*.

Bad days happen to everyone, especially during long periods of unemployment. Doubt inevitably creeps in. But don't let it derail your strategy. Stick with it until you have clear, rational reasons to change direction. Ruts are mental traps, not reflections of reality. Once you pull through, you'll see there was nothing to worry about — you were just overthinking.

Once out of the rut, you'll see that nothing has fundamentally changed. It was your mindset that needed adjustment. Stay focused on your goals, even when the path seems unclear. When the time for a strategy change comes, make sure it's driven by logic, not temporary feelings.

6   Individuality getting hammered by social pressures

I moved back to my parents' place right before my unemployment began. At 31. There's nothing inherently bad about living with your parents as an adult, especially for financial reasons. I wouldn't have to pay rent, utilities or other bills as long as I helped out with chores and small tasks.

While this arrangement saved me a lot of money — hundreds of euros each month — it quickly became clear it wasn't ideal. I felt incredibly grateful to my parents, but within the first week, I realized it might've been a mistake. Though I had my own small room with a door, it didn't shield me from the constant interruptions. The dogs barked so often that I could barely hear my own thoughts.

Like many adults who return to their parents' homes, I felt a lack of privacy and my individuality seemed constantly infringed upon, even though my parents didn't mean to. Noise was something I could tolerate, but the real issue was how little privacy I had. When I was working, I could focus on my daily routines and coding with total clarity. Now I had to react quickly to my parents' requests and rush to help or respond.

Initially I was frustrated, unable to focus as intently as I once did. But after a couple of weeks I learned to adapt. I could code again, even if I had to deal with interruptions. It wasn't ideal — I'd lost some privacy and focus — but I adjusted. I accepted the situation as it was and tried not to be too hard on myself. I also made an effort not to disturb anyone, recognizing that it was only fair to contribute something for my free accommodation.

I fit my household chores around my job search and other tasks. I made my meals during the day when the sun powered the solar panels, using the electricity that would otherwise be sold for a pitiful price. I got used to my father's moralizing and frequent comments about my 'laziness': "I've been working all day cutting firewood, but no one else was around!"

Usually I was up by 7 am, woken by the dog's barking. I did my writing at night, after my parents went to bed, constantly feeling a bit sleep-deprived. At times like that I was grateful not to have my own family to manage. I could barely handle my parents.

Parents often treat their children as though they never left when they move back in. You start to wonder how they managed without you doing all these tasks. Did they think I was lazy unless I had a constant to-do list? Personally, I would prefer to live more like a tenant than a dependent family member. The boundaries between parent and child blur in this kind of setup, remnants from childhood. I love my parents, but I'm not a child anymore. I don't need constant inquiry about what I'm doing or why — I'm an adult who doesn't need permission or approval to live my life.

I know my parents are proud of my achievements, the degrees I've earned and the skills I've developed, but there's still a part of them that sees me as their child. They acknowledge what I've done but don't seem to recognize that I did it through my own choices and initiative. It's hard to maintain your individuality when others want to fit you into a version of yourself that you've outgrown. You need to find support and knowledgeable people elsewhere, otherwise you're not going anywhere and won't be able to follow your personal goals and dreams.

I've always been close to my parents, and they haven't changed much over the years. Their days revolve around work, small projects and routines. It's a simple, steady life that repeats day after day. They don't understand what it's like to voluntarily push yourself to grow, to put yourself in challenging situations to improve your skills and knowledge.

Unfortunately, when it comes to pursuing personal passions, family support often falls short. It's easy to end up living a double life — working on your passion in secret because it's not acknowledged as 'real' work. You end up doing twice as much: working to satisfy your family's expectations while pursuing your own goals in the background. It's mentally and physically exhausting, like holding down two jobs.

I've had two passions since I was a child: computers and reading. I used to read a lot of Donald Duck comics, much to my father's dismay. "Are you reading again?" he'd ask, as if it were a waste of time. Yet, reading is what helped me get into university and earn three master's degrees.

I also loved computers and gaming. But to my father, gaming was just another waste of time. Coding was considered "useful," but he still saw it as unnecessary. In his eyes there's no real work to be done on a computer, even though everyone is quick to ask for my help when they have tech issues. I'm the household "tech support," but there's no respect or appreciation for the effort it took to gain these skills. Once my father asked why Windows had suddenly switched to English.

I didn't bother explaining that it hadn't; something else had probably confused him, but there was no point in getting into it.

Now that I'm unemployed my father seems to think it's his role to supervise my job search, bombarding me with endless questions. It's that Protestant work ethic kicking in — you're only valuable if you're working. I'm trying my best, but it doesn't help that he's dismissed nearly every ambition I've ever had.

7   Self-confidence

Morgan Housel says in his book *The Psychology of Money* that "[s]aving money is the gap between your ego and your income [...]". That is such a wonderful and true statement. There's also a gap between your ego and your dreams which is comprised of self-confidence and humility. Without humility you can't build on your mistakes or realistically assess where you stand in relation to your goals. Without self-confidence you'll never be able to take that decisive step when no one else can do it for you. This leads to inaction, often accompanied by hesitation.

It's common to see people confident in certain areas of expertise while lacking confidence in others. Overconfidence is a reflection of a person's healthy or unhealthy narcissism. However, it's rare to see people who are truly narcissistically overconfident — I don't know anyone who fits that description. More often it's the opposite. Most people I know doubt themselves and say "I can't do this" or "I'm not capable of that".

My parents never directly told me I couldn't do something, but I've noticed how their lack of confidence, likely passed down from their own parents, has influenced them. People who lack self-confidence also lack vision — they can't see the connection between their actions and their ability to improve their situation.

I discussed this with my mother once and she said, "Joni, you took such a big step when you went to university [...]". She was referring to me being the first in our family to go to university (if you don't count my aunt who went to Sibelius Academy). It was an automatic, unreflective reaction, rooted in the mentality that such an achievement is rare and highly valued. When you've accomplished something considered significant, people often stop there — they fixate on that milestone instead of thinking about the future. It reminds me of the song by Jennifer Lopez, *Jenny from the Block.* My version would be: 'Don't be fooled by the degree that I got, I'm still, I'm still Joni from the middle of nowhere countryside and a member of working-class folks who lack all confidence'.

These days, going to university in Finland isn't rare — over 40 percent of younger generations have a higher education degree. My mother's reaction came from the perspective of a previous generation, when attending university was far less common, especially in our part of Finland. But while times have changed, that old mindset remains.

Having a university degree means more to my parents than it does to me. For years they couldn't even say what I was studying and after I graduated they could barely remember my majors. I have three master's degrees, none of which guarantee me a steady job. Now I compete with people who don't necessarily have the right degrees but were born at a time when a degree wasn't an absolute requirement.

I know universities aren't holy institutions, but working-class people often compare their families by the number of degrees earned. Fathers take pride in their educated sons, but they also feel ashamed of their own lack of education. And it's understandable — a generation ago more education meant better job prospects and higher pay. But that's no longer a given, as every young unemployed and highly educated job seeker knows all too well.

The greatest tragedy is that those who are insecure and indecisive lack confidence in learning. The world is constantly changing and those who can't learn or adapt are left behind. Lacking confidence in learning means lacking confidence in your options: the belief that you can't leave your current job, can't learn new skills and can't change when change is necessary.

Self-confidence, by its nature, requires a certain amount of blindness. We all know our limits — we may even feel the pain of those limits. But when we are confident, we have to ignore those limitations and imagine ourselves capable of achieving things we haven't yet accomplished.

When we are confident, we put ourselves in the position we want to be in within our mind's eye. This confidence acts as a bridge between who we are now and who we want to become. For example, if I want to be courageous, I should act and appear courageous. If I act and look courageous, others will believe I am courageous and eventually I will believe it too. This creates a positive momentum, where everything I do aligns with the idea of becoming courageous.

Courage is most needed at the beginning, when change is hardest. Perhaps what we fear most is the change within ourselves. But once we begin, fear takes a back seat and we simply don't have time for it anymore.

8   Balanced unemployment

Whatever you do during unemployment, one thing is certain: you need daily routines and a balanced mix of activities to keep you motivated and productive. Balanced unemployment means applying for jobs, but also ensuring that your life remains interesting and fulfilling. Once you've completed your daily job search tasks, allow yourself to enjoy life's small pleasures and disconnect from the job hunt. You can't speed things up by overworking yourself.

At this stage, you don't even know if your current efforts will result in a job or if you'll land the dream role you've been hoping for. The best approach is to continue following your strategy, while working on your weak points and enjoying life as much as you can along the way.

If you feel a nagging sense that something is off or that a significant skill gap might hurt your employability, take the time now to address it while you still can.

Keep your options open and explore areas close to your expertise. For example, if you're a front-end developer, consider expanding your knowledge into related fields like graphic design, UX design or even back-end development. This way, when you eventually attend interviews, you can confidently say you've been actively growing your skill set and broadening your expertise. You might even come across opportunities where these newly acquired skills become immediately useful.

You don't need to spend hours applying for jobs when a 30-minute check of new listings might be sufficient. There are significant cultural differences in how much time job seekers spend on their search. In Finland the average job seeker spends about one hour per day on job-related tasks, while in the United States it's closer to three hours. There are likely many reasons for this, including Finland's smaller job market and longer average employment duration, which contrasts with the faster-paced U.S. job market. Regardless, don't spend more time than necessary. If you're spending three hours a day browsing listings with no substantial results, you might need to reassess your strategy.

No matter where you are, increase your chances by applying to several positions, but don't apply to jobs that don't fit your expertise. For example, if you're an electrician, don't waste time applying to a beauty salon. You can send out a few applications each day, but focus on jobs you can genuinely see yourself working in. This will save you both time and energy.

Always keep your job search strategy in mind. With a clear vision, you can concentrate on areas that need improvement. Found three job postings that match your skills and interest you? Great, apply to all of them. Noticed something missing in your resume? Fix it. Feel like your Excel skills need work? Take a course and enhance those skills.

When you keep your eyes and mind open, countless interesting opportunities are waiting for you. Choose a few of these and work on them once you've completed your daily job search tasks.

9   The unemployed hustle

As an unemployed person, I've had countless ideas about what could help me out of my rut. I often find myself brainstorming ways to turn all the 'L's into 'W's. My first thought? Money. I considered diving into coding to make money, freelancing, picking and selling berries, saving more aggressively, learning to trade stock options or even filling out surveys for spare change.

While some of these might lead to useful and lasting opportunities, many are just distractions. Taking on an interesting coding project or earning a bit of cash by selling items can be fun, but unless you're fully committed these activities are best suited for when you're already employed. Selling items worth 10% of your monthly rent or starting a project that takes months to complete may not be the most effective use of your time.

It's not bad to explore your options occasionally, even when you have a steady job and everything seems to be in order. We should all take time to brainstorm and jot down our ideas. There's no shame in our desires and dreams, though they can sometimes be a bit daunting or obscure.

Here's a list of roles I mentally explored at the beginning of my unemployment:

- Writer

- YouTuber

- Streamer

- Student (doctoral studies)

- Student (coding)

- Businessman (own business)

- Employee (sport governance)

- Employee (telemarketing and other suitable roles)

- Freelance coder

- Futures/arbitrage trader

- Globetrotter

Looking at this list, I feel different emotions for each option and various thoughts come to mind. For instance, the term "writer" resonates with me since writing has always felt natural. Throughout high school I received top marks in Finnish language tests.

I always thought writing could be enjoyable, but I'm hesitant about writing in English and am not interested in mainstream fiction. The Finnish market is small and I worry I won't get noticed. I've seen talented writers go unrecognized. I also worry about making mistakes in English as I once had a reviewer lower my grade for errors in my writing. Despite these doubts, here I am, writing in English and trying to push past the criticism.

One realization from this list is that my ambitions aren't particularly bold. There are no grandiose goals like becoming the President of Finland, owning a multi-billion euro company or curing cancer. Most of these roles are within reach and could potentially be pursued within a year, at least as a hobby. This insight suggests that I might be thinking too small. If something is achievable within a year, it's within my grasp. This perspective makes it harder for me to come up with excuses. I feel a strong need to act immediately because I can no longer justify my procrastination.

10 Act before you're ready

Many social media influencers and YouTubers offer advice to aspiring influencers, often summarizing their guidance with the phrase: "Act before you're ready". I agree with this sentiment, though not because of their advice. I have my own reasons and a story to share.

In business literature it's often said that you should make your first offer while you're still embarrassed. After university I worked in telemarketing because I couldn't find any other job. It was initially very embarrassing. When I started calling people, I wasn't ready, and the only thing that kept me going was the script that I had. Everyone who started without previous experience felt just as embarrassed and scared as I did. But it changed me.

I was never a top salesperson, but I gradually became more confident and relaxed on the phone. I started focusing on the needs of the person I was speaking to and made constant offers. During my brief telemarketing career I sold everything from car union memberships to electricity contracts, tablets and mobile connections. Most of the things I sold were actually good deals.

It was hard work. I was often cursed at and rejected, but I learned that ego doesn't matter in this line of work. Resistance from prospects was common, but some customers bought despite verbal attacks and insults. There were times when the prospects changed their minds so quickly that I barely realized they wanted to buy.

In telemarketing, the rule is: the sooner you forget your last disappointment, the better. Whether your last prospect was a buyer or not, you need to move on to the next call. Experienced telemarketers are relentless, presenting all the positives about the product while downplaying the negatives — sometimes even the truth.

Despite the harsh environment, full of self-reproach and self-encouragement, I respected every worker who put themselves on the line and came to work day after day. My time in telemarketing taught me a lot and gave me a new perspective — a business perspective. A businessman acts before he's ready, lets go of his ego and remains receptive to all customer needs and signals. I learned that being a businessman doesn't mean doing a perfect job; remarkable results can come from trial and error. I made many sales when I wasn't ready and could barely communicate, funny as it sounds.

Telemarketing changed my life, but I still wasn't fully embracing the advice to "act before you're ready". I realized that it's possible to be courageous in one area of life and still be timid in others. Then, one day, I had a revelation while reading Steven Pressfield's *Turning Pro* (2012). He discusses how he wanted to be a writer but struggled to start working. There were always excuses and resistance. Eventually he overcame it and began writing regularly. After finishing his first book, *The War of Art*, he said:

> "The [first] manuscript didn't find a publisher and it shouldn't have. It wasn't good enough. I had to go back to a real job, in advertising in New York, and save up again, and quit again, and write another book that also didn't find a publisher because it also wasn't good enough. Neither were the nine screenplays I wrote over the next X years, I can't even remember how many, before I finally got my first check for thirty-five hundred dollars and promptly went back to writing more screenplays that I also couldn't sell".

After reading that, I thought, "Wow, this man wrote and wrote, nine screenplays and more! That's true grit!" I imagined him stacking typewriter-written manuscripts in his desk drawer, surrounded by unsold novels and screenplays, while he kept typing away.

His early writings were probably not great, but he remained consistent. Slowly he grew into his role, enjoyed the process and realized he had to keep going. He said:

> "In the end I answered the question [What's wrong with me?] by realizing that I had no choice. I couldn't do anything else. When I tried, I got so depressed I couldn't stand it. So when I wrote yet another novel or screenplay that I couldn't sell, I had no choice but to write another after that. The truth was, I was enjoying myself. Maybe nobody else liked the stuff I was doing, but I did. I was learning. I was getting better. The work became, in its own demented way, a practice. It sustained me, and it sustains me still".

While Pressfield doesn't explicitly say "Act before you're ready", his journey illustrates the idea. Being ready isn't about the work itself; it's about facing your own limitations and starting anyway. When Steven began working relentlessly, he felt like he was "truly facing his demons, and truly working his shit".

So why should you "act before you're ready"? Consider this: Steven wrote almost obsessively, never feeling fully "ready". He embraced the journey despite never being ready to be a distinguished writer.

You can apply this lesson to all tasks. Imagine yourself as a pro, embarking on something new and adopting a professional mindset. This technique involves adjusting your mental reference points, reducing the gap between yourself and a true professional. By acknowledging the mistakes they've made and the efforts required, you remove excuses and begin acting like a pro, starting today.

For instance, if you're a writer, aim to write 20 books before considering yourself ready. If you're a coder, develop at least 20 full-stack apps. If you're a musician, aim for 10 albums. It will take time. The best time to start was yesterday and the second best is today. So why not start today?

Once you begin acting, "everything becomes simple". Take this advice from Steven. Once you start, you no longer need to wonder if you're 'ready'.

11 Intermediate level

If you want to be successful in what you do, you need to bring enough value. That usually means reaching at least an intermediate level. Being a rookie is not enough; you need to "turn into a pro" as writer Steven Pressfield says. If you have a marketable degree or valuable skills, you have a head start compared to those who don't, but having a degree doesn't make you a pro if you're still unemployed and not taking responsibility for yourself or your actions.

Turning into a pro is not just about doing things, it's a mindset. You cross the line between being an amateur and a professional. Before you might have been trying things half-heartedly, but now you push yourself and take real risks. You start talking the talk and walking the walk.

Getting to an intermediate level isn't easy, especially if you don't have a proper education. If you've tried marketing yourself online, you know how tough it can be. Don't compete in online business unless you really know what you're doing or if the opportunity costs are low. The only reason for someone unemployed to hustle is that opportunity costs might be low. You need to assess these costs and trade-offs to decide if it's worth it. When I was unemployed, I had nothing to lose and trying new things had a lot of upside and little downside — that's what led me to write this book.

There are plenty of talented people who can do amazing things and might work for less. Most of the time online hustling isn't worth the time investment. If you don't have advanced skills yet, you have a better chance of success outside the online world. I'm not trying to discourage you, just giving a realistic view.

I've tried so many online hustles looking for easy money that I've lost count and dropped them when I realized they weren't worth my time. I couldn't evaluate my chances realistically and that was probably my biggest mistake. There are millions of people trying the same thing. If there's easy money, it's usually only available for early adopters. Eventually it's no longer easy money for anyone.

To succeed, you need an edge. YouTubers might say it's easy, that you can succeed on your first try, but it's not. We don't know how many people have failed trying the same thing.

Think about what sets you apart. Is it your skills or your determination? For me, my writing is what differentiates me. Everything else depends on willpower.

When searching for freelance gigs online, you'll see plenty of people with intermediate or advanced skills. I was looking for freelance coding jobs in Finland and found that the listings were often specific. Companies want problem solvers. Small businesses often look for turnkey solutions — not just a pretty website but one with registration, data collection and a proper database. Once you can do these things confidently, you'll be able to find coding work.

Work becomes easier once you've found your place. Your skills will reach a level where you can count on getting regular gigs. Or if you manage to get a 9-to-5 job, you'll have a stable workplace where you don't need to justify yourself constantly. If you're an entrepreneur, you'll build a client base that trusts you and enjoys working with you. This is the reward for the effort and hardship.

Unemployment or feeling useless often comes from not bringing enough value to others. You haven't started being a pro. You lack passion and initiative. If you were bringing enough value, you wouldn't be in this situation or feel depressed because you'd know you can generate value elsewhere.

A pro doesn't allow their thoughts to be scattered. You stay focused because you know you have a mission that aligns with your vision. And even if your vision isn't clear yet, you keep working until your mission turns into one.

12 The unemployed businessman

The best time to start acting like a businessman is when you're unemployed. I really mean it.

First, your opportunity costs are probably very low. You're not giving up a €100,000 annual salary for unpaid self-improvement (opportunity cost: -€100,000). If you were working full-time, part-time or in a more complicated situation, your opportunity costs would be higher – you'd have to sacrifice something in exchange for your growth. Plus, when you're unemployed, you likely have more time on your hands. In any other situation, you'd probably have less.

The second reason to start thinking like a businessman is your need for business-related skills. You should begin developing those skills right away. If you're starting from scratch, I recommend Josh Kaufman's *The Personal MBA* (2010), which covers everything you need to know. You also need to adopt a business mindset. Think and act like someone in business. If you don't have family or friends in business, read inspiring stories of entrepreneurs. Don't focus only on making money, but look for insights into how successful entrepreneurs connect with their businesses. Derek Sivers' books are great for this. *Anything You Want* (2015) and *Hell Yeah or No* (2020) offer entertaining and insightful perspectives on running a business.

Derek Sivers, founder of CD Baby, says you don't need a grand vision or plan to become an entrepreneur. His advice is to "stay focused on helping people today". That's where you start. Ask yourself: how can you make someone's life a little better? Once you can answer that, you'll know what to do – start adding value and your life will move in a better direction.

If you're pursuing a traditional job, first decide your personal business strategy. What is your product? What's your brand? How would you describe yourself if you were the product?

You need to know what employers want, how the market – in this case, the job market – works and how to establish your personal brand credibly so employers will seek you out. How do you market yourself and your skills? What sets you apart from other job applicants?

Ask yourself: what am I trying to achieve? A new job? What kind of job? A business of my own? A lifestyle with multiple income streams and varied but interesting work? You may want to keep your options open, applying for jobs while leaving room to start side hustles or a business.

If entrepreneurship is your goal, start developing your "minimum viable offers" as soon as possible. Josh Kaufman defines this as "an offer that promises and/or provides the smallest number of benefits necessary to produce an actual sale". You need to determine the minimum conditions required to make a sale – the basic product or service that turns your expertise into income. Begin by pitching your ideas. You might feel unprepared, but don't let that stop you. Even if your product isn't ready, ask people if they'd be interested in buying what you plan to offer. If there's enough interest, you can start with presales, gauging demand before taking on too much risk.

This concept also applies to employees working on side projects or prototypes that might one day turn into a business. Even the most brilliant invention could be forgotten without proper marketing. Destiny's grace isn't secured by intelligence alone, but through effective promotion.

Learn to market what you offer and you'll be more successful than you would be otherwise.

13 Mission statement

Whether you're opting for the entrepreneurial route or seeking employment, you need to be able to state your mission clearly. Derek Sivers says you don't need a vision or plan to succeed, but you do need to know what you're doing. You should be able to state your mission in one phrase and build your strategy around it. You don't need to share it publicly; it's enough that you know what it is.

Since I'm focusing on the employment route, my personal mission is to "secure a position as a sports secretary or similar role with a salary of at least 2,800 euros per month". I'm the product, and my goal is to market myself to potential customers (employers) at a price I believe they are willing to pay for my services. My vision is to continue working in the field of sports administration, gradually progressing to more demanding, fulfilling and better-paid roles.

With my mission clearly stated, here's a concrete example of how I've been progressing my 'business strategy'. I graduated from university in 2019 with three master's degrees: one in philosophy, one in sociology and one in the social sciences of sport. It was clear from the start that I had to make myself marketable using the latter. Although I studied sports from a societal perspective, employers weren't interested in that focus. I had a knack for writing, but I didn't feel inclined to pursue a doctoral program (let alone what came after), so I chose a more practical career path.

What did I do? I began emphasizing my professional identity as an expert in sports administration and governance. More specifically, I focused on my knowledge of local municipal governance, highlighting that in my job search. And guess what? It worked. I landed my first real job as a sports secretary in a small municipality in eastern Finland. Before that I had only done telemarketing and a short three-month training stint in municipal sports services.

If I hadn't emphasized my skills in practical governance, including project management, communication, people skills, administration and stewardship, I wouldn't have succeeded. I had to believe in myself even amid constant rejection and failure and fine-tune my approach. What got me the job was a stroke of luck – I was offered a fixed-term contract as a substitute because there was simply no one else available to do it! I realized that my success wasn't due to me being better than other candidates; I may have been the least experienced. But that didn't matter.

I worked in that position for almost two years and suddenly my market value soared. I applied for various jobs during that temporary post and discovered that getting a new job was easier than I'd thought. I was no longer seen as a rookie; I'd climbed to an intermediate level. Now I was a young professional with a promising career ahead. That small taste of success – thanks to one fortunate opportunity – was enough to change everything. It was my first successful asymmetric bet in the job market.

Now I'm unemployed again, but things are different. I know what worked last time. While the same strategy might not work this time, I have a solid frame of reference. I understand how the market functions, though conditions might be a bit different now. My strategy worked before, so I'm trying the same approach with slight tactical adjustments. I'm applying for jobs with slightly more demanding requirements. Most of my applications should match the listed qualifications. My goal is to secure interviews for at least 20% of the jobs I apply for. If my success rate drops below 10%, I'll know something's wrong and that I need to adjust my approach.

As a realistic businessman I know the odds of success. In my age group (25–34), 75% of people secure a job within the first six months of unemployment, assuming the economy is stable. But times are tough now and the number of job postings has decreased compared to last year or even a few months ago. (At the time of writing, it's late summer and job listings have been sparse for several months.) These are external factors that no one can control. All I can do is refine my approach or change my strategy if necessary. I need to stay informed about changes in the world, keep up with the times and continually revise the feedback I get from the market. Aside from that, I must prepare for hard times, be kind to myself and accept that economic life has its fluctuations.

Economists talk about a lack of supply for jobs or something along those lines. The reality is that it's harder than usual for the unemployed, with more qualified applicants competing for fewer jobs. On top of that, the Finnish government is tightening its budget, leading people to hold onto their jobs more tightly than before. The non-governmental sector is also struggling to generate new employment. The healthcare sector is the one area still hiring, but even that is at risk of cuts and layoffs.

I may have to adjust my expectations of finding a job within the first six months of unemployment as the odds for my age group and the broader workforce decline over time. Lower expectations don't mean I need to change my strategy; they simply mean that the asymmetry in the market is increasing – there are fewer winners and more losers and the stakes are higher.

14 Were you raised by an employee or an entrepreneur?

I grew up in a nuclear family with my parents and brother, where my parents embodied the traditional Protestant work ethic. Both of them were employees for most of their lives, with my father in particular demonstrating a strong dedication to hard work. However, as my brother and I grew older, we began to see a rift between their approach to work and our emerging sense of a more business-oriented ethic. While there's nothing wrong with working hard, we began to realize that quality, value creation and strategic thinking were often more important than the simple act of hard work itself.

The Protestant work ethic, as I've come to understand it, has two major flaws. First, it encourages people to work for the sake of work, measuring their worth and success by how much they do, rather than what value they create. If you don't work enough or aren't as capable, you're seen as a lesser person. This approach diminishes the difference between should and could. People may take on work that lacks purpose or value just to meet an arbitrary standard. This is akin to saving money with the hope of becoming a millionaire — it's a rational action, but it doesn't align with the larger goal. Working for the sake of work can be just as ineffective, leading to exhaustion without achieving meaningful results.

I've seen this mentality in action — people breaking their bodies in grueling jobs, taking pride in how much they suffer for the sake of work. But this is misguided. There's no valor in ruining your health just to prove you can work hard, especially when that work doesn't bring real rewards or fulfillment. Hard work shouldn't lead to an early grave.

The second issue with this ethic is that it places too much emphasis on doing things for others simply because it's expected. Helping others can be rewarding, but only when it's motivated by genuine personal desire, not societal pressure. Too many people sacrifice their well-being to meet other people's expectations, often without realizing how much it drains them. The focus shifts from value creation to meeting social norms and obligations, which can lead people down paths they didn't choose.

This traditional mindset still lingers in Finnish society. Working-class families, like mine, often hold onto the dream of owning a large house, a big yard and even a summer cottage. But this dream comes with an overwhelming amount of work — work that doesn't generate value, knowledge or financial gain. It feels like pure madness. The endless chores prevent people from pursuing goals that might actually improve their future.

This mentality, rooted in a history of farm labor just a few generations ago, still shapes how people think about work today. My grandparents worked on self-sustaining farms and even my parents helped with farm work as children. These experiences formed unconscious patterns of behavior that my parents continue to follow. As a result, many children are raised with the expectation of getting a steady job, just as their parents did, and they feel the pressure to meet these expectations even when they want something different.

The divide between generations becomes clear when we talk about work. Many young people feel that their parents don't understand how difficult it is to find a job or earn a living wage today. Our parents can only show us what they know — how to be employees. But they can't always teach us how to navigate the complexities of today's job market or how to succeed as entrepreneurs. It would be great if parents taught their children both paths, but that rarely happens.

Schools are trying to address this gap. When I was a child, we were asked if we wanted to be entrepreneurs. At the time, none of us did. But today entrepreneurship education is more common and I imagine students would be more open to the idea now. There's been a cultural shift in how we view entrepreneurship, but it's still in contrast to Finland's long-standing tradition of strong unions, lifelong employment and job security. This has created a rigid labor market where employee rights are prioritized, but this rigidity has its downsides.

Strong employee rights come at a price. The comfort and security that long-term employees enjoy contribute to an inflexible job market that leaves many unemployed. I experienced this firsthand as an employer representative in a situation where I couldn't even issue a warning to an employee who committed multiple severe infractions. This was due to financial incentives that made it more costly to address the issue than to let it slide. In a truly efficient market, such problems wouldn't exist because employees would be replaced based on performance, but the public sector often can't operate this way.

The private sector, on the other hand, must be more flexible to survive, firing underperforming employees and adapting quickly. Sometimes I wish the public sector would adopt more of this mentality to eliminate inefficiencies. The current system breeds stagnation and it's largely due to the employee mindset that dominates public sector organizations.

Watching my brother start his own business recently has given me new insight into the entrepreneurial mindset. It's exciting and full of possibilities and I can see how this energy is contagious. I've been considering starting my own business as well, seeing firsthand the fulfillment and satisfaction that comes from taking control of one's work life. Many people, disillusioned by rigid workplaces, turn to entrepreneurship to find freedom and purpose. It's rare to see the reverse — an entrepreneur choosing to become an employee.

In the end it's about balance. We all inherit different attitudes about work from our parents, but we also need to adapt to the changing realities of the job market and our own evolving aspirations. Whether we embrace the entrepreneurial spirit or the security of steady employment, the key is to ensure that our work aligns with our personal values and long-term goals. For me, that means working smart, not just hard.

15 Waiting for retirement

In Finland it's common to hear working men joke about their retirement. They might say, "Oh, I wish I could retire", "It's about time for me to retire" or "I should retire.".[6] These comments are often meant to amuse, but they also reflect a genuine preoccupation with retirement while they are still working. I've always found these remarks a bit distasteful, especially when they come up multiple times a week.

I've observed many people retire, and often their last day at work seems like any other. There might be a bit of cake during a coffee break and some tense but kind farewell speeches. Other than that, retirement day is generally just like any other day, albeit with a bittersweet undertone.

The process of retirement in Finland can feel somewhat abrupt. When people retire, it often feels as though their presence is swiftly erased from the workplace. New employees who join shortly after might barely know the retirees ever existed. Retirement in Finland typically occurs in one's early sixties, sometimes closer to seventy. According to

---

[6] These men clearly lack protestant work ethic. A true man of work would never joke about retiring.

the old-age pension calculator, my pension could start as early as September 1, 2060, giving me 36 years to wait. If I live to the expected life expectancy, I would have 22 years and 7 months to enjoy my pension.

The Finnish pension system is largely funded through taxpayer money and partially from pension insurance funds. All employees contribute a portion of their salaries to pension insurance, while current workers and taxpayers fund the pensions of today's retirees. The sustainability of this system relies on a continuous flow of workers and taxpayers as the contributions from past generations are insufficient to cover current pensions. For example, women born in the 1940s receive seven euros for every euro they contributed, according to Statistics Finland. While societal affluence allows for this imbalance now, it may not last indefinitely.

Future workers might pay more in contributions than they receive in pensions. This imbalance reflects the current system's design, where those with higher incomes have better retirement benefits, while lower-income workers might find their pensions insufficient. Even with 30–35 years of work as a cleaner or janitor, the pension may not be significantly higher than that of someone who never worked.

How is that possible? Well, first of all, there just aren't enough accrued withholdings from a cleaner's or janitor's salary. A lot of money from every paycheck goes to taxes, either through straight withholdings or later through different taxes: there are value added taxes, inheritance taxes and so on.

The guarantee pension, currently capped at €976.59 per month, is a safety net for those who haven't accumulated enough pension contributions.[7] While this amount might cover basic living expenses, it's insufficient for a comfortable life, especially if a pensioner requires expensive private care or lives in a costly city. The guarantee pension does not stretch far in these scenarios.

Guaranteed pension is not enough when a pensioner has to use expensive (private) sheltered accommodation, which can cost more than €7,000 per month in intensified treatment units. Even if you find relatively cheap sheltered accommodation, it could still cost at least €100–150 per day. In more expensive rented apartments, particularly in larger cities, the costs can easily exceed one's means.

Pensioners form a significant voting bloc in Finland. As a result, the pension system is strongly protected by law. Politicians are generally cautious about proposing major changes to the system and often opt for adding new benefits rather than addressing potential future shortfalls. This political inertia helps preserve current benefits but may not fully address the challenges that could arise down the line.

Should I be concerned about my own retirement at this point in my life? The high cost of elderly care suggests that I should indeed be worried about the cost of living for pensioners, both

---

[7] Guarantee pension is calculated with formula: 'Guarantee pension minus other pensions' (inc. national pension and employee pension).

for myself in the future and for those currently retired. I have no reason to eagerly anticipate retirement unless I can consistently earn enough to support myself in the future. Predicting this is challenging unfortunately. I can't be certain whether the pension system will maintain its current inflation-adjusted levels or preserve purchasing power over the decades. Given the current economic trajectory, it's more likely that pensioners will face greater difficulties in the future unless there are significant economic improvements.

While the future is always uncertain and 36 years is a long time to wait, it's sensible to plan for retirement, regardless of your age. Planning becomes increasingly important as you approach retirement age. The most compelling reason not to worry excessively about retirement right now involves shifting our perspective on the concept itself. Retirement, as a distinct phase of life, is a relatively recent invention. Historically people worked, lived and loved until they died. If we could all lead healthy lives and find meaning in our work, concerns about retirement would be less pressing. Longer lifespans don't always translate to a fuller life as many struggle with health issues that diminish their quality of life.

Social democratic reforms introduced the idea of retirement as a separate life phase, meant for fulfilling postponed dreams and desires. While it's reassuring that Western countries have robust systems for elderly care, I wish it didn't cast such a bleak view of the future. I want to experience and achieve many things before reaching retirement age rather than waiting until then to live fully.

An alternative approach is to incorporate "mini-retirements" throughout one's career, as suggested by Timothy Ferriss in *The 4-Hour Workweek* (2011). Although I haven't tried mini-retirements myself, the idea makes sense: instead of deferring life until retirement one can take several months off work each year. Whether by quitting a job or negotiating time off with an employer, this strategy allows for periodic breaks that can offer a fresh perspective on life and work. Many people who take such breaks find that their mini-retirements become more rewarding over time, providing clarity on what truly matters in life.

As I reflect on these aspects of retirement, it's crucial to recognize the inherent risks and uncertainties involved. The possibility of dying before reaching retirement age would render years of contributions moot. Unlike investing, where one has some control over decisions, pension contributions are managed by pension funds with limited personal oversight. Additional complications, such as moving abroad, could further complicate pension plans.

Given these uncertainties, it's essential to approach the idea of retirement with a realistic perspective. While it's important to plan for the future it's equally vital not to fixate solely on the notion of retirement as the ultimate goal. Exploring private pension options that offer greater control and flexibility might be a more prudent approach. Managing contributions based on personal income and needs could be a more adaptable strategy than relying entirely on a system that may not guarantee the retirement you envision. Balancing current enjoyment with future planning, rather than deferring all dreams to retirement, could lead to a more fulfilling and secure life overall.

16 The job interview mindset

> "If you are unsure of a course of action, do not attempt it. Your doubts and hesitations will infect your execution. Timidity is dangerous: Better to enter with boldness. Any mistakes you commit through audacity are easily corrected with more audacity. Everyone admires the bold; no one honors the timid". – Robert Greene, *The 48 Laws of Power,* Law 28

Every job interview should be approached with boldness and confidence. If you can't go into an interview with assurance, it might be better to skip it. If you're uncertain about the fit, don't force it. Employers who are truly interested in you will overlook a bit of nervousness, but you might regret taking a job if you're not fully sure about it.

You can't lose by being confident. Even if you don't have an answer to every question, respond with conviction and maintain your composure while thinking about your next answer. Act as though you have multiple other options. This mindset, though challenging, helps you stay cool and level-headed. Remember, accepting a job offer means trading some flexibility for financial security — there's always a trade-off.

You should act as if you had a dozen other options waiting. I know it's hard to do, but I'm saying this from a rational standpoint. You have options. You keep your options by staying cool and level-headed. Remember: If you come to an agreement with the employer, you get the money and you lose your flexibility; you win money and feeling of security, but you lose your time and you lose your options. It's a trade-off, no matter how you look at it.

I've experienced butterflies in my stomach before every significant interview. The nervousness can be overwhelming, but it typically subsides once the interview starts. While nervousness is natural, it's crucial not to let it affect your performance. Nervousness before the interview is fine as long as it doesn't undermine your confidence during it.

An interview is essentially a power struggle with established norms: answer questions, stay focused, confidently present your accomplishments, ask insightful questions if time permits and then wait for the outcome. It's impossible to gauge how an interview went from the interviewer's perspective. Sometimes you think you've nailed it only to hear nothing and other times you feel your performance was lackluster only to receive a callback.

I've had a few bad interviews where the interviewer seemed disinterested or even disrespectful. It's disheartening. After a couple of such experiences, it's very tempting to quit. However, it's important to get past these setbacks and continue with new interviews.

Never take the outcome personally. Both you and the interviewer are doing your jobs. If you stay professional, there's no shame in losing out to someone else, even if they're less qualified. Factors beyond qualifications might influence the decision, such as internal candidates or personal preferences. You can always ask for feedback, but don't expect employers to disclose the full truth about their decision-making process. Keep your chin up and be prepared for the next opportunity. Remember that every interview is a step towards finding the right fit. Stay positive and be ready for the next opportunity. And don't forget that there's still plenty of upside ahead.

17 It's up to the employer to decide who to employ

Ultimately the decision of who gets hired rests with the employer. If you find it difficult to accept this reality, you might want to consider entrepreneurship as an alternative.

When you're job searching, accepting this fact is crucial. You mustn't let the employer's decisions, attitudes or even potential biases, such as racism, affect your mindset. When faced with rejection or setbacks, draw from ancient Stoic wisdom to remind yourself: "I've lost nothing. This is only a failure if I choose to see it that way. My success should be measured by my inner calm, not by external judgments".

Letting yourself be upset by rejection is understandable if financial concerns are at play, but beyond that it's important to recognize that you and the employer are primarily pursuing your own interests. The job search is a transactional process; the employer needs someone to fill a role and you need compensation. If you can't find common ground, another candidate will, and that's simply part of the process.

In Finland, the rigidity of collective labor agreements often limits negotiation flexibility. Salaries are typically predefined according to these agreements, especially in the public sector, where the lowest possible salary is often offered. Employers may inquire about your salary expectations just to gauge if they can afford you and if you're willing to accept the lowest bid. If you're not willing, they might find someone else who is. Providing a salary range and referencing market standards can help demonstrate your awareness of industry norms without pricing yourself out of contention.

Career coaches recognize that many highly competent candidates never secure positions due to various factors. In the U.S., for example, automated systems and high volumes of applications can overshadow deserving candidates. While Finland's job market has fewer applicants, it still faces challenges. Excessive qualification requirements often hinder career flexibility. For instance, even roles like preschool caretaking may require advanced degrees, making career changes and job transitions more difficult.

Remember that the job market's inflexibility and stringent qualifications are beyond your control. Focus on presenting your best self and aligning your skills with opportunities where you can add value without being disheartened by the factors you cannot influence.

18 Downside, downside in my mind

"I gave up on applying for a tech job in 2023 after two years of numerous job application attempts and interviews that went nowhere. It's more effort than it's actually worth. I have a comp sci degree with a professional certification (which was costly to take). [...] If you're financially restricted like I was after post grad. It's time to give up your dreams, wake up to reality and apply for other jobs. Because sitting, indulging yourself in self-improvements/projects and waiting around for a callback is the worst decision you can make! It's a surefire way to be homeless since weeks turn to months and before you know it you're down on your last 500$ in your bank account".

This is what a YouTube commenter, Brian Lai, writes about his job search experience. I was watching a tech job market video one evening and was deeply touched by his story.

Brian aims to warn other aspiring software engineers and tech graduates about the dangers of betting heavily on a tech career. His honesty and courage are commendable, as many shy away from discussing the risks and setbacks associated with high-stakes career bets. His experience is likely more common than we'd like to admit. With fewer tech jobs available now compared to just a couple of years earlier, Brian's story serves as a reminder that even well-qualified candidates can face significant hurdles.

Brian's two-year job search didn't yield the results he hoped for. Although we don't know every detail of his efforts or the specifics of his situation, it's clear that the investment in his degree and job search was not paying off. He described his job search as "more effort than it's actually worth", indicating that his bet on finding a tech job was no longer justified.

Later I'll offer actionable advice on how to avoid Brian's situation. His main issue was treating his job search as an all-or-nothing bet. He invested heavily in his degree, which created pressure to succeed despite the challenges. As his financial situation worsened, the stakes of his bet became increasingly high, making it harder to continue.

If you find yourself in a similar predicament, remember that there are always more than two options. For Brian, giving up on his dreams entirely was not the only solution. A viable third option is to step back, take on any job that helps cover your expenses and continue working towards your dreams when your situation improves.

Brian's problem wasn't just "sitting, indulging himself in self-improvements/projects and waiting around"; it was the negative cash flow, a narrow path and insufficient preparedness for financial setbacks. Even during tough times it's possible to stay engaged in skill development and pursue relevant opportunities without excessive waiting.

It comes down to evaluating the expected value of different options. If the value of continuing on your current path is too low compared to other possibilities, it's reasonable to pivot. "Waking up" to the low expected value means recognizing when it's time to change direction before facing complete financial devastation. Each of us has a point where the risk of a failed bet outweighs the potential reward. It's important to know when to reassess and adapt.

19 Best for you is not best for me

There's a recurring thought I have while unemployed: that ultimately I am the only one who can truly help myself. I alone know what I need and what's best for me. It may sound simple, but it's not.

Analyzing societal incentives reveals constant tension and contradictions. For example, a clerk at an employment service might be more interested in quickly closing your case than in your long-term well-being. Meanwhile you might want to escape unemployment quickly but not at the expense of settling for any job just to get by. There's a conflict between your interests and theirs, as well as those of policymakers who often prioritize quick fixes.[8]

Your future employer wants the best candidate, but this might not align with your own interests or what you discover about yourself once you're in a job. Reality is shaped by past

---

[8] Politicians often claim that the unemployed are lazy and that it's in their best interest to remain unemployed. If that were true, there wouldn't be such a need for moralizing. I don't subscribe to this moralizing because I can't see how it would be in the best interest of the unemployed to stay unemployed long-term.

incentives and decisions. We are often led to believe that our interests align with those of others. But no one shares your exact interests.

Consider what would happen if everyone followed the same advice or had the same interests. The market would become distorted and inefficiencies would proliferate. For example, if everyone rushed to buy stocks based on one advisor's recommendation, the stock prices would inflate unrealistically, making everyone appear rich but ultimately leaving us with inflated values and diminished purchasing power.

Societal balance is maintained by individuals pursuing their own interests. While unemployment might be bad from a societal standpoint, it's unclear if it's universally detrimental or beneficial for any specific individual. Even in my own life, it's hard to determine if being unemployed today is good or bad in the long run. People will have strong opinions on your situation, but outcomes often vary more at the individual level than at the systemic level.

Even when it comes to my own life, I have no way of knowing if being unemployed today is good or bad for me in the long run. Many people you encounter may have strong feelings or opinions about your unemployment. There's usually more variance in outcomes on an individual level than on a systemic level. There's more strength in saying 'We're fucked' when the dysfunction is systemic rather than when it affects an individual.

Remind yourself of this next time you start wondering whether what you're doing in your personal life is right by the standards of society. Society can endure a significant amount of dysfunction, so what you're doing with your time and money on an individual level is quite insignificant. Social comparison should be the least of your worries. The bottom line is to do only what feels right to you.

There are plenty of things that don't fit right with me. For example, if I were a good writer, I would automatically renounce all options to become a journalist. Why? I might be able to meet all the standards of journalistic requirements, but even then I couldn't make myself believe that I should feed people useless nonsense all day long. We need journalism, good journalism, but I don't want a life where I constantly ask myself: 'What's the point in all of this?' and write yet another pointless piece about interest rates or whatever this or that person said.

Another occupation that doesn't fit right with me is being a psychologist. I've studied psychology in high school and university and have always been interested in psychological research, but I've come to realize that working as a psychologist would be a nightmare. I have no interest in solving other people's problems and what's worse, I wouldn't be able to convince myself that my patients need me or that what I'm doing is useful. I have no faith in the Diagnostic and Statistical Manual of Mental Disorders (DSM), depression treatments or ADHD assessments. I lack confidence in a culture that tries to solve mental health issues by creating an army of psychologists, each with their own vested interests, which diminishes their ability to offer genuinely beneficial recommendations.

Many jobs require me to lose both my rational thinking and my individuality. I was watching a morning show on TV the other day (I rarely watch TV) and there was a lady talking about how prescription-free medicine shouldn't be sold in ordinary markets. Yes, that would be the natural conclusion if you're a representative of the union of pharmacists.

Then there's the head of a labor union who says that raising the salaries of practical nurses is in the common interest and that nurses are 'in a wage pothole' compared to other professions. Yes, when you're a union head, you would believe that, no matter what. These people were selected as representatives with ideal characteristics. I don't believe for a second there will ever be enough evidence to convince them that they might be wrong. I would love for all of us to have fat paychecks, but when I look at the economic data, I can't help but conclude that high wages benefit mostly certain groups (members of unions, protected and prestigious professions, etc.) while the invisible downside (unemployment) is correspondingly and unknowingly directed to the less fortunate. What is best for the profession of practical nurses is not necessarily best for me, other workers, other professions or even the unemployed.

It is sad that work life can be like that. Not only do you need to do your job, but you should also carry a certain ideology with you.

I remember when I was studying sport administration and social sciences of sport nearly 10 years ago, I wrote in one assignment essay that one thing I really liked about sport sciences was how apolitical these sport fanatics seemed compared to students of social sciences or even to students of philosophy.

I've had it easy since the only ideological requirement in my profession is to believe that physical activity is good for health. That kind of ideological commitment is lightweight compared to other commitments you might have to endorse in your work organization. As a professional in sport services and administration, I have had no difficulties admitting that it can be rationally justifiable to allocate money to objectives other than sport and physical activity. I don't think my sector is always treated as well as it should or given enough money for necessary repairs or investments, but I would have no quarrel with investing scarce resources towards basic amenities rather than using them for a new sports facility or a swimming hall, for example.

What bothers me most in public sector work and as a civil servant myself is the misuse of scarce resources and the inefficient use of taxpayer money. Every organization has its own way of handling money allocation, but money is cheap when you're a government worker in a high office. My department (sports services and youth services) used resources extremely sparingly in my previous job (no investments were made), but the allocation of resources wasn't as tight at a higher level.

Let's say there's an idea about a new project supported by the highest political leaders or governmental directors. It could be a new building, a new project or a new job position in an organization. Once there's enough political support and enthusiasm, there's nothing you can do about the fact that the project is a gross misuse of public funds and shouldn't even be discussed, let alone commenced if the common interest of taxpayers were considered. I have no political affiliations, but I feel uneasy whenever I think about the inefficiencies I've seen in the public sector. Nothing is easier than using other people's money for projects where you have nothing to lose personally.

I never thought that resources would be allocated efficiently through a tax-based public system, but reality proved to be scarier and the government more irrational than I could have imagined. When I think about it, I always remember a story from economist Thomas Sowell. He was a vehement Marxist until the age of 23 or 24 until he realized he couldn't maintain his Marxist ideology against the hard facts of reality. He says: "What one summer working for the government as economist was enough to show me that the government was really not the answer [...] And I realized these guys [top officials of labor department, -JP] are not gonna save us".[9] Sowell warns about governmental policies that are meant to be helpful but can in fact cause harm or the precise opposite of what they were intended to do. Studying under Milton Friedman was not

---

[9] Thomas Sowell in an interview. **Why I quit being a Marxist | Thomas Sowell**. Watched on Youtube 26.8.2024. Hyperlink: https://www.youtube.com/watch?v=HpCm6mOu0MU

enough to change him, but one summer job at a government post was.

Nassim Nicholas Taleb is another scholar and writer who has criticized the public misuse of resources with similar arguments. According to him, "[b]ureaucracy is a construction by which a person is conveniently separated from the consequences of his or her actions".[10] When action is separated from its consequences, actions do not return necessary feedback, and because of that, interventions might add excessive and inefficient complications. He also says that "[t]hings designed by people without skin in the game tend to grow in complication (before their final collapse)." It is not good for society to have lots of people in government positions without any personal skin in the game. If a lack of skin doesn't 'collapse' society, then at least it will make our lives more miserable through indirect consequences.

There are many respects in which I don't agree with Sowell or Taleb, but their criticism of the inefficiencies of the public sector is as relevant and important now as ever. The public sector here in Finland has grown enormously and is probably one of the reasons why we haven't seen good economic growth in many years. Recently I read that only the public sector has been able to grow here in Finland for the last couple of years, considering all hires in both public and private sectors in a given year. The private sector hasn't been able to produce

---

[10] In his book *Skin in the Game: Hidden Asymmetries in Daily Life* (2018).

new jobs at all while the public sector has been growing, partly due to the increasing need for health and elderly care.[11]

Many people don't realize that there's always a payer for inefficiencies, whether in the public sector or private sector. For example, inefficiencies in the job market are paid by taxpayers as a whole. Some benefit from a rigid system (those with protected jobs) while others suffer greatly (the unemployed, for example). But when you consider all these inefficiencies across different sectors, you can be sure that we are all paying for it, one way or another.

I want to mention one example from my own profession. People can do sports without public support and exercise either on their own or by using private services. Public services are most cost-effective when the user would not be able to buy the service on their own and there is no private market that can provide it. A swimming hall is a great example. It would be too expensive to build your own swimming hall and no business would provide that kind of service if there isn't enough market demand and earning capacity. Setting up a public swimming hall funded mostly (subsidized) with taxpayer money is a great way to provide cheap services for

---

[11] I'm not an economist, but I can still point out that the number of jobs alone does not provide a precise understanding of how the economy is performing. For example, in Finland we might have a high employment rate at a certain point in time (though currently it's not high at all), but this can coexist with a large number of people outside the active workforce. Thus, the economy might still not be booming despite a high employment rate. The total number of hires can be growing while the number of people outside the workforce is also increasing.

those who need them, but it comes with the caveat that the benefit is not distributed equally. Those who use the service get more than their money's worth (because it's publicly subsidized), while those who don't use the service are essentially wasting their money in paid taxes.

The baseline in service production should always be that the service provided is produced as cheaply as possible and only if people are willing to pay for it (or have the service tested against differing interests). When I work as a public servant in the public sector, it is in my interest and in taxpayers' interest to make sure services are bought as cheaply as possible. If we neglect efficiency, the cost will eventually fall on someone — possibly even on me — because we haven't ensured that services are delivered effectively.

Public services can still be valuable, but we must remain vigilant about the inefficient use of resources. While public services do not always match the cost-effectiveness of private services, they offer many merits that justify their existence. However, when taxes are collected for redundant or unnecessary purposes, it undermines their original intent. It's akin to having a neighbor making decisions with my money without regard for my interests. In the worst-case scenario, managing taxpayer money can resemble shopping for a neighbor.

In public sector work, how resources are allocated is often based on past decisions, contracts, habits, pressures from political and administrative leaders and existing infrastructure. Future allocations might continue to follow these patterns, but I advocate for decisions grounded in careful cost-benefit analysis, needs assessment and rational evaluation rather than political expediency or whims.

Administrative work often lacks a realistic perspective on how to allocate funds across different sectors. Few people can effectively compare options to determine the best value. Financial managers may understand the numbers but often lack the practical expertise to make meaningful comparisons.

Despite the challenges and inefficiencies in public sector work, I can still see myself working there. I am confident in my abilities as a public servant and take the efficient use of resources very seriously. It's unfortunate that I can't easily demonstrate this aspect of my work to employers and it's equally disappointing that they often don't prioritize it.

20 Who is responsible for unemployment?

Unemployment is both a necessity and a common tragedy. The blame falls on both the individual and society, though not equally. Unemployment is never chosen — it is an identity forced upon people.

From a societal perspective, unemployment is a necessity because the job market wouldn't function efficiently without job transitions. Job switching involves friction: workers come and go, enter and leave the workforce, firms lay off and recruit new employees and so on.

A Finnish philosopher[12] once argued that those who have jobs should be grateful to the unemployed for allowing them the privilege of work. He meant at least two things: some workers and the unemployed are interchangeable in the sense that they have similar skills and the outcomes could have been different (roles reversed) and there are not enough jobs to go around even when considering workers' skills and other factors.

Currently there are approximately 226,000 unemployed individuals in Finland (official numbers from June 2024; the actual number may be higher) with a total population of 5.6 million. In July 2024 there were only 48,200 open job positions and 306,000 people searching for work. Even if each open position were filled, we would still need 257,800 more positions for those left without work. Many positions are filled by immigrants and some remain unfilled. Heikki Räisänen from the Ministry of Economic Affairs and Employment of Finland estimated in 2018 that 15,000 jobs remain unfilled annually because employers can't find suitable candidates.

Eliminating unemployment with minor political changes is unlikely when large-scale structural issues are at play. In July 2024 there were 98,600 unemployed individuals who had been job searching for over a year. Many of these people are at risk of permanently leaving the workforce. Extended unemployment weakens the chances of finding work.

---

[12] A philosopher named Jukka Hankamäki, in his book Työttömän kuolema (written in Finnish), discusses these issues.

If the goal is to place the unemployed in existing jobs, it seems like a 'mission impossible' given the constraints. Those with jobs might feel moral indignation towards the unemployed for receiving benefits while they work, but it's clear that there aren't enough jobs to go around.

I don't have a solution for how Finnish society could resolve high unemployment, but I suggest that improving job market efficiency is key. This means creating strong incentives for the unemployed to accept jobs and for employers to create them. Immigration is not a solution because there aren't enough competent and Finnish-speaking immigrants. While smart and hardworking immigrants can be beneficial, accepting them in large quantities may only delay problems or create new ones that a small country might struggle to manage.

Increasing job market efficiency through societal interventions is possible to a certain extent, but determining the optimal solution for reducing unemployment is complex if not impossible.[13] Forcing highly educated individuals into any available job is not an efficient use of resources.

Political parties have differing views on the nature of the problem and potential solutions. Finnish left-wing parties often lack a deep understanding of economic mechanics. Right-wing parties, while more economically knowledgeable,

---

[13] I suggest interventions only because they've been used in the past. I'm neither for nor against interventions, but I don't believe this society could remove previous ones without introducing new measures in their place due to the strong resistance such changes would face.

may be blind to normal people's incentives. They often use a 'stick method' — penalties without proper incentives — which can be counterproductive. For instance, reducing unemployment benefits is meant to improve the incentive to work, but it's doubtful that spending cuts will do more than increase resentment among the unemployed and fear among those who might lose their jobs.

The unemployed already face significant disadvantages: they bear the risks of unemployment while the employed enjoy their rewards. Many employed individuals don't face much risk while many unemployed struggle to stay afloat. In Finland, every euro earned during unemployment reduces the unemployment benefit by 50 percent. It's unclear how such incentives will reduce unemployment.

The existence of unemployment benefits may not be inherently moral, but it reflects the reality that market interventions in the job market often lead to high unemployment and significant risk. When negotiations between the unemployed and employers are restricted by strong regulations, a public insurance fund where all employees contribute is necessary. Employers also contribute, which is a clever system in Finland for alleviating systemic risk.

21 Luck is always involved in business and life

The results in business and job searches are always partly determined by luck. Many YouTubers claim in their thumbnails that there's no luck in success — a common but misleading notion. It's irresponsible to suggest that luck isn't involved. These creators should focus on their skills and achievements rather than dismissing the role of luck.

While incredible intelligence and willpower can lead to success, it's misleading to ignore the influence of risk and chance. Many aspects of our lives are shaped by factors such as where we were born, our parents, our intelligence and other physical attributes.

Even if we could control these factors, external influences still play a significant role in luck. Today's world is increasingly controlled by algorithms. Algorithms, which are mathematical shortcuts designed to simplify processes, can remove many real-life variables that might otherwise affect outcomes. Algorithms simplify processes but also eliminate variables that could affect outcomes. For instance, algorithms might screen job applications based on predefined criteria, removing many real-life factors.

When dealing with algorithms, luck plays a role that we cannot control. Algorithms tend to favor those already identified as winners, making it harder for others to succeed. Even with the best skills, you might still be overlooked.

Luck applies to job search and business, as well. Successful actions in work life and business seem definite only because they are examined 'after the fact'. Successful actions were rarely known before they became successful for the first time. The mentally perceived link between actions and results is hindered by "causal opacity" (in Taleb's words), which means that in many cases cause and effect can't be known for certain due to the many variables involved.

We could ensure that luck is not a factor only if we could simulate reality accurately by running controlled experiments with known variables and symmetric (deterministic) phenomena. When inputs and outputs are asymmetric and researched phenomena are non-linear, we cannot ascertain what will happen for sure, as even the smallest asymmetry can skew results and introduce instability into the system.

There are many known unknowns and unknown unknowns[14] that could jeopardize whatever you start, even if you manage to control the process. You might have a perfect business operation with everything under control, but suddenly something unforeseen could come along and wreck your plans. Taleb calls these events Black Swan events. They can be small or large but are always unexpected.

For example, a known unknown could be a lack of customers. You don't know if you will have enough customers, but that's an unknown you can imagine. Unknown unknowns are more pernicious. You can't see them coming and you can't even imagine them because they have never happened to you

---

[14] United States Secretary of Defense Donald Rumsfeld once said that "there are known knowns; there are things we know we know. We also know there are known unknowns; that is to say we know there are some things we do not know. But there are also unknown unknowns — the ones we don't know we don't know. And if one looks throughout the history of our country and other free countries, it is the latter category that tends to be the difficult ones".

before. You might not have any hint about them, even remotely. You can easily envision a destructive fire, a lack of customers or bankruptcy, but it's harder to foresee regulatory changes, cyberattacks or sudden losses of personnel.

Getting fired can be a small Black Swan event that's a known unknown. If your employer suddenly files for bankruptcy, you might lose your job instantly. Losing a job can happen quickly, but on most days we believe our jobs are safe. Whether getting fired is good or bad depends on the next steps in our lives, which are also partly determined by luck.

In a nutshell: life is partly determined by luck, but we have no way to accurately measure how lucky or unlucky we are at any given moment. We might be at our luckiest or unluckiest point without knowing it. All you can do is maximize your opportunities. You don't need to see where you stand because you can always protect your options and enhance your luck, regardless of how luck comes to you.

Part 2

Increase your chances for success

All right. Before I conclude this book, I want to leave you with some concrete tips. Here are 13 pieces of advice you should consider, especially if you're unemployed but also if you're looking to add more rationality to your life and increase your chances of success.

1   Write down your goals

Having clearly defined daily and long-term goals is essential. Without them you risk drifting aimlessly. Writing down your goals helps you understand yourself better — who you are, where you've been and where you want to go. The more precise your goals, the better.

Here are some of my goals:

- Secure a position as a sports secretary or comparable role with a salary of at least 2,800 euros per month within the first six months of unemployment.

- Exercise at least every two days and maintain a healthy diet.

- Write at least one page every day in the 'Jobless Diaries'.

- Check job listings daily and apply immediately if something interesting comes up.

- Read at least a couple of pages each day.

- Keep improving your coding skills — next goal is to experiment with linear gradients on canvases and implement them on websites.

- Improve YouTube thumbnails.

- Complete the NextJS tutorial you started.

- Take out the trash, vacuum all rooms and clean all monitors and desktop computers.

It's okay to mix short-term and long-term goals. The important thing is to articulate what you believe is worth striving for. Revisit these goals regularly and assess which ones still feel relevant after a few weeks of effort. Once you've built a strong habit around a particular goal, you might even drop it from the list as you no longer need a reminder.

When a new goal emerges, write it down and revisit it after a few days to see if it still resonates. Cross off any goals that no longer seem important or that you've completed. Periodically reviewing your list helps you track your progress and identify tasks you haven't started or finished. If you find yourself resisting a certain goal, ask yourself whether it's something you truly want to pursue. If not, remove it and reassess your other goals. Is it just one goal that no longer aligns with your priorities or is there a broader shift happening?

If your goals are related to job searching, write them down and reflect on how your goals and actions align. Are your goals realistic, concrete and manageable? Are you being too hard or too lenient on yourself? Are these goals expanding your options, improving your market value and enhancing your skills?

> 2   Define your strategy and parameters for failure and success, then stick to that strategy and only change it when absolutely necessary

Your strategy can be anything that moves you closer to your goals, but it should always put you in a better position than where you started. The key is to have clear criteria for success. Remember that goals may fail, but the strategy can still succeed — you just won't know in advance which goals will work out. It's entirely possible that you might leave many of your goals unmet but still find your strategy successful overall.

For example, as I've mentioned, my current main goal is to "get a job as a sports secretary or in a comparable position with a salary of at least 2,800 euros per month within the first six months of unemployment". If I don't achieve that, I'll know I've failed at reaching my goal, but not necessarily in executing my strategy. My overarching strategy is to succeed and thrive in life. If that goal doesn't pan out, I'll adjust the goal while maintaining the strategy. Why set the six-month mark? After that point I'll have to start applying for jobs that employment services assign to me to retain my benefits. But sticking to my strategy could still be worthwhile even then. I'll comply with the public servant's requirements, but I can continue to pursue jobs that align with my interests and skills.

Right now I'm prepared to wait until I've exhausted all unemployment benefits, which cover the first 400 weekdays, before considering a major change to my strategy.

If you were to ask me later about my strategy, things may have changed. I could discover new opportunities or ways to generate income before my benefits run out.

However, one thing is clear: I won't let myself end up in a position where I have to rely on reduced unemployment benefits. If nothing else works out, I'll pivot and start a business or find another way to make money honorably. That's where I draw the line.

3   *Make a concrete plan of how you are going to make money in near future*

Previously we learned from commenter 'Brian Lai" who experienced bad luck and setbacks in his job search. He warned us about the dangers of "sitting idle, indulging in self-improvements or projects, and waiting around", especially when we're running low on funds. No one can sustain negative cash flow forever.

It would be great if we all landed our dream jobs with the financial security that comes with them, but that's not the reality for most. We need backup plans in case things don't go as expected. So I want you to create a concrete plan for how you'll make money if your unemployment persists. This exercise is beneficial even if you're employed because it expands your mental horizon and helps you focus on areas that could yield the most financial benefits.

Start by listing your options in order of likelihood, with the most likely at the top. How realistic is each option for making money? Be honest with yourself. You should also estimate the potential monetary impact of each option — how much do you expect to make? Write down all your expected income sources and add an approximate timeline for when that income could start.

If you think your future self might consider taking entry-level or part-time jobs, instead of continuing the search for a perfect match with your expertise and education, include that option as well.

Here's an example of how you could do it:

Description	Time	Impact	Probability
Unemployment benefit	July - December 2024	High	High
Part-time job in telemarketing	January 2025 -	Medium	Medium
Berry business	June - September 2024	Medium	Medium
Freelance coding	Four times a year	Small	Low
Arbitrage betting	-	Unknown	Very low
Hedge fund manager	Asap	Huge	Very low

A person in this example has been unemployed since July and will receive unemployment benefits until the end of year. He hasn't landed his ideal job yet so he brainstorms different ways to earn money. Knowing he's a skilled communicator, he considers taking a job in telemarketing, even though it's not what he hoped for. At the very least it will cover his bills when his benefits run out. Meanwhile he continues searching for a better job and refuses to give up on his dreams.

Now that you've hopefully made your list of income options, take a close look at each one. Ask yourself: *How can I improve my chances of success with this option? Are there any opportunities I haven't yet considered?*

Finally, get to work. If you're running out of money, focus on the most viable options and pursue them until your financial situation improves. Then reassess your list of options. I recommend revisiting this exercise at least a couple of times a year.

4   Use the method of approximating expected value

In Essay 2 I discussed my target salary and in Essay 13 I mentioned the chances of success in job searches for my age group. These variables, along with many others, are important when estimating the chances of success. The key is to use data to your advantage. In every developed country there are plenty of statistics about job seekers, market trends and economic conditions that you can tap into to form a realistic picture of your situation. Using data helps you approximate expected value and make more informed decisions.

Although calculating the exact expected value of a job search is difficult, in many cases a betting formula can be applied:

(Expected amount won * probability of winning) – (Amount lost * probability of losing)

If someone could search for jobs indefinitely without depleting their financial resources or damaging their reputation, they might choose to apply only when the expected value is positive, aiming to win in the long run. What complicates matters is that in job hunting the potential loss (e.g. time, reputation, finances) and the probability of losing increase as unemployment continues. This is why it's vital to track the changes in your expected value over time, adjusting strategies when necessary.

The expected value is usually highest in the early stages of unemployment, so remaining vigilant and aware of shifts is essential. As time goes on, expected value often drops. It's important to recognize when this happens to avoid being blindsided by negative outcomes. Even if you don't succeed right away, using data to guide your actions helps you understand whether your decisions were sound based on the conditions at the time.

In short, utilizing data for approximating expected value is a crucial part of managing job searches effectively, allowing you to adjust strategies based on realistic assessments and trends even when external factors — like luck — are unpredictable.

5   Never evaluate your actions 'after the fact'

It's easy to fall into the trap of evaluating your decisions in hindsight. Let's say you started a new business, but it failed due to a lack of customers. You blame yourself, thinking you should have anticipated the low demand and done better research. While it's true that learning from mistakes is important, hindsight assessments are often misleading.

There are two key reasons why evaluating your past actions this way is unhelpful. First, you could never know for certain what the future holds, no matter how much research or planning you did. Second, your perspective is skewed because you're judging past decisions with the benefit of information you didn't have at the time. This creates a gap between how you assess the situation now and how you should have approached it in the moment.

The goal is to make balanced and informed decisions when they count, not to punish yourself after things go wrong. To do this, imagine how you or someone else might view the same decision 20 years in the future. Would you make the same choice? Would a mentor or someone you respect agree with your decision? If, at the time, you did your research, weighed your options and made decisions without being swayed by short-term pressures, then there's no reason to blame yourself when things don't turn out as expected.

Hindsight thinking often leads to statements like "I should have known" or "I saw this coming", but in reality most situations are far more unpredictable than we like to admit. Judging past decisions with the knowledge of outcomes distorts your ability to learn in a healthy way. Instead of focusing on past mistakes, aim to make rational and thoughtful decisions in real-time and let yourself off the hook for what couldn't be foreseen.

Learn from the past, but be kind to yourself. Don't carry unnecessary blame for things you couldn't predict.

6   Maximize your options

Having options means that you have a possibility to do something in the future (according to your interest) but you have no obligation to do so. Having options is important, because we can't see into the future and we can't know for sure what we want in the future.

If we could foresee the future, there would be no need to keep options open — we'd focus entirely on what's coming and take full advantage of that knowledge. Similarly if we always knew exactly what we wanted, we wouldn't need to worry about regret. We would be able to make perfect judgments about our desires and needs in any given situation and compare them with absolute clarity. Having options means that even without certainty about the future or ourselves, we can still make rational decisions in the face of uncertainty.

Can you have too many options in life? Of course — it can be overwhelming. But more often the issue is having too few options or not recognizing the ones that exist.

Consider a rough patch in life: you're broke and just lost your job. Being broke means having limited financial options — you can't meet even urgent needs. That's a tangible problem. And with the loss of your job, two issues arise. The first is literal optionlessness: you simply aren't creating enough options for yourself. The second is that you're not recognizing the options you do have. Those options exist, but for some reason they're not on your radar. You can't maximize your opportunities unless you can see them.

Maximizing options often equates to maximizing your luck. The difference between lucky and unlucky people isn't just circumstantial. It's not that some are inherently lucky or unlucky. Often it is the case that lucky people make themselves lucky by believing in their potential for luck. This belief allows them to see opportunities others might overlook and by choosing those options they increase their chances of success. Does that make sense?

Sure, there are people who face genuinely unlucky situations they can't control. But many people unwittingly contribute to their own bad luck and then attribute their misfortunes to fate.[15] In reality, much of our bad luck stems from actions or patterns that expose us to unnecessary risk. We just don't always see it.

7   Learn from experience and refine your approach

Remember that you're not bound by your past actions. If you feel compelled to stick to a well-trodden path, you may be limiting your options. There could be more effective ways to achieve your goals.

---

[15] David Schwartz refers to this phenomenon as 'luck excusitis' in his book *The Magic of Thinking Big* (2016). He describes it as a self-defeating belief where a person genuinely believes that they cannot be lucky or successful. Schwartz demonstrates in his book how adopting the right beliefs can lead to true success.

If you're in desperate need of money, the method of acquiring it may not be as important as the fact that you find a way. If you're seeking more job interviews, consider tweaking your CV or marketing yourself for adjacent fields by slightly adjusting the description of your expertise.

Don't feel confined to traditional roles in your field. For instance, if you're a construction worker and there are no jobs available, don't despair. Skilled workers are always in demand; you just need to find the right opportunity.

If you have a side business that's thriving, it might be worth considering a full-time switch. If you can succeed in your own venture just as well as you do in your current job, why not be your own boss?

Sometimes experience will lead you to realize that your current path isn't viable. That's okay. Many people bravely pivot to entirely new careers, and this kind of courage can be admirable. Once you decide to change careers, avoid looking back. Embrace your new direction fully and let go of the past.

If your current approach is working, there's no need to change what doesn't need fixing. For example, after becoming unemployed I considered revising my CV. However, since I was receiving interview calls with my existing CV, I continued using it without modification. If something works, there's no need to fix it.

8   Light a fire under your ass, the right way

If you're unemployed and out of savings, you probably already have a lot of motivation by necessity. Even if you're not in dire straits, it's crucial to create and manage your own sense of urgency.

Robert Greene, author of books like *The 48 Laws of Power* (2000) and *The 33 Strategies of War* (2006), uses the metaphor of "death ground" to describe a powerful way to drive action. Greene recounts his experience working in Paris, where he had to learn French quickly or face leaving the country. Despite his introversion and embarrassment, he pushed himself to master the language. This high-stakes environment forced him to act and discover capabilities he didn't know he had.

When faced with high pressure, like having a family to support or being stuck in a dead-end job, you're more likely to succeed because you put yourself in a situation where failure is not an option. You create your own "death ground" where the only outcome is success or enduring the same unfulfilling situation.

It's important to balance this pressure with responsibility. Your family and obligations come first. They'd prefer you to find a sustainable way to improve your situation rather than risking everything.

One effective method to create this kind of pressure is by setting deadlines. Make them ambitious but realistic. For example, if you estimate that creating a website will take a week, challenge yourself to complete it in three days. This urgency can prevent distractions and keep you focused.

Use this method judiciously. It's not suitable for every task, especially those that benefit from a more measured approach. Learning, for instance, can't always be rushed. Yet applying deadlines to tasks where possible can enhance focus and drive.

Consistently applying pressure through deadlines can lead to a fast-paced, fulfilling life. For those prone to depression, staying occupied with high-intensity projects can be a powerful way to stay engaged and avoid negative emotions.

9   Be careful with comparisons

Social comparison is often said to be a path to dissatisfaction. People frequently yearn for what they perceive others possess — money, fame, status or a loving family. While comparing yourself to others isn't inherently negative, it's crucial to be mindful of the impact it has on your life and well-being.

To improve the quality of your life, compare yourself to those who embody the virtues or success you aspire to achieve. Aim to adopt their standards and qualities, not merely their possessions or status. Remember that many successful individuals have reached their positions through various means, including luck and favorable circumstances, not solely through personal excellence.

Virtuous people are admirable because they embody qualities that lead to genuine fulfillment. They are not swayed by the actions of others but focus on living a life of virtue. Their strength lies in setting a powerful example, showing that true happiness often comes from living virtuously rather than seeking external validation.

When comparing yourself to others, ensure it's not driven by jealousy. Jealousy can cloud your judgment and lead to negative feelings. Let admiration guide your comparisons. By setting high standards for yourself and drawing inspiration from those who excel, you can feel energized and motivated. Competence breeds confidence, and this newfound confidence can make your goals seem more attainable.

Use comparisons with those less fortunate as a tool for gratitude. Reflecting on the challenges faced by others can help you appreciate what you have and remind you of the harsh realities some face. In some Russian prefectures unemployed men face severe consequences, such as being sent to war under threat of losing benefits. Such comparisons can help you recognize the value of your current situation and foster a sense of gratitude.

By carefully managing your comparisons, you can harness their potential to motivate and inspire rather than to discourage or diminish your sense of self-worth.

10 Read to increase your optionality

When you're unemployed, it's essential to immerse yourself in knowledge that enhances your skills and increases your options. Focus on resources that offer practical advice and can be immediately applied to your situation. Shakespeare and other classic literature can wait; right now, you need tools and insights that can help you improve your circumstances and create opportunities.

Consider reading books and articles that address your specific needs. If you're struggling with managing finances, seek out materials on personal finance and budgeting. If you need to improve your daily habits, find books on productivity and habit formation.[16] For those interested in personal branding or entrepreneurship, delve into business and startup guides. If job interviews are a challenge, explore resources dedicated to interview techniques and preparation.

For example, if you're a coder, concentrate on advanced coding techniques and mastering the fundamentals of your

---

[16] I highly recommend *Atomic Habits* (2018) from James Clear.

chosen programming language. If you have a side hustle, investigate strategies for scaling and improving your earnings by studying successful business practices in your sector.

If reading isn't your preference, consider watching tutorials or listening to podcasts related to your field. But remember that passive consumption is different from active engagement. Watching and listening can provide insights, but applying what you learn through hands-on practice is crucial. For coders, experimenting and tweaking code based on what you've learned can significantly enhance your understanding and skills.

In essence, reading and engaging with relevant material can empower you to increase your optionality and give you a competitive edge in your job search and personal development.

11 Protect yourself from downside

Unemployment brings its own set of challenges, but the real trouble begins when various downsides accumulate. While being unemployed is difficult the situation becomes much graver if it leads to a cascade of other issues — such as financial ruin, deteriorating health, loss of support or even homelessness. Though these extreme outcomes are unlikely, they are not impossible and recovering from such a situation is extremely challenging.

It's crucial to take proactive steps to mitigate risks and avoid letting chance dictate your fate. Prepare yourself for potential setbacks by asking: Are you ready for significant disruptions? Consider the following scenarios:

- A major health crisis that prevents you from working.
- Loss of essential resources, like bananas or coffee, due to supply chain issues.
- Interruptions in basic services, such as water, internet or electricity.

For instance, I once experienced a two-week power outage due to a severe storm. It was a tough experience that underscored just how crucial preparedness is. If you're not ready for small inconveniences like that, there's a high chance you're not ready for bigger disappointments either. And in reality, you probably underestimate how quickly bad luck can come your way.[17]

---

[17] Probabilities are hard to fathom for a normal human being. One classic example of how people miscalculate their chances is that the dangers of air traffic are overestimated and the risks of highway

Even minor setbacks can become overwhelming if you're not adequately prepared. Reflecting on past events, like Finland's wartime hardships, highlights the importance of readiness. While the likelihood of something extreme like war may seem low, having contingency plans and basic emergency supplies can provide a sense of security and resilience.

Accidents and disasters can strike anyone, regardless of circumstances. The conveniences we enjoy today can also make us more vulnerable to unexpected disruptions. Black Swan events — those rare, unpredictable occurrences — are an inherent part of our interconnected world. Being prepared for them, even in small ways, can make all the difference.

I have to admit that I, too, have room for improvement when it comes to crisis preparedness. But ensuring that you're ready for small disruptions can strengthen your resilience for larger challenges ahead. It's not about paranoia — it's about safeguarding your stability and well-being in an unpredictable world.

12 Be patient

Understand that your chosen strategy can only be executed at the pace dictated by reality. If you're aiming for significant

---

traffic are underestimated (due to the illusion of control and skewed presentation of accidents portrayed in the media, in this case).

rewards, you'll need to accept that achieving them often requires more risk, greater asymmetry and most importantly more time. Patience is crucial; without it, you may unintentionally limit your potential for success. Good things rarely arrive on our timetable. They come when they are ready and being patient allows you to capitalize on opportunities as they arise.

If you're searching for the best job fit, recognize that finding it may take longer than expected. The job market is full of variance — despite your efforts and qualifications, outcomes can differ significantly. Some individuals secure their ideal job within three months, while others may take 18 months, despite having similar talents and work ethics. This disparity often comes down to luck and timing.

While waiting 18 months might seem daunting, consider whether it would be worthwhile if it meant landing your dream job. For something truly exceptional, the wait might be well worth it. Embrace patience as a necessary part of the journey towards achieving your goals.

13 Get ready to disappoint others

This tip may seem disheartening, but it's essential to face reality.

During unemployment, you might find yourself inundated with requests from close relatives or friends who assume you have ample time and should fulfill their needs. Despite your best efforts, you will inevitably disappoint some of them. It's important to recognize that this is a normal part of navigating your own priorities and limitations.

Ichiro Kishimi and Fumitake Koga's book *The Courage To Be Disliked* (2019) offers valuable insights into handling rejection and managing others' expectations. If you struggle with the idea of letting people down, this book might provide some comfort and perspective.

Understand that you cannot satisfy everyone's wishes. Attempting to do so can lead to a never-ending cycle of new demands and increased stress. Remember that people are resilient and can handle disappointment. Your self-respect and the quality of your relationships are not solely dependent on meeting everyone's expectations.

For example, I once faced a situation where my father asked for my help during a particularly busy time for me. I explained that I couldn't assist him immediately and he took offense, leading to a week of strained communication. This experience taught me that it's important to set boundaries and manage others' expectations about my availability. My time and attention are valuable and it's crucial to prioritize my own needs while offering help when I can do so genuinely.

Disappointing others is often a minor inconvenience for them but a significant source of stress for you if you constantly try to meet every expectation. It's better to set clear boundaries and communicate your limitations respectfully. Doing things for others only when you truly want to, rather than out of obligation, ensures that your actions align with your own happiness and well-being.

Recognize that it's impossible to avoid causing some disappointment and that's okay. Prioritize your own needs and be mindful of how you allocate your time and energy. Balancing your responsibilities and your own well-being is crucial for a fulfilling and stress-free life.

Epilogue

I've shared a lot about the experience of being unemployed in these diaries. You might be curious about what became of the writer in the end. Let me share my story with you.

The beginning of my unemployment was challenging. My journey started in June, following a promising job interview in May while I was still employed. Despite my hopes I ended up in second place for that position and didn't secure a job before my unemployment began.

The initial three summer months were particularly tough. As expected, job postings dwindled during the summer and I soon discovered that new job postings had nearly halved compared to the previous year. Many other job seekers, including myself, faced a similar struggle. Employers were overwhelmed by the volume of applications, making it a highly competitive market.

After the first three months of unemployment it felt like I was stuck in a rut. Despite increasing calls for interviews, I had little success. It seemed as though my efforts were in vain. Around this time I became incredibly proactive, driven by the desire to achieve something before the year ended.

In addition to working on this book project, I launched a YouTube channel named *Branching Business* and created several channels for YouTube Shorts. One of these channels, dedicated to Finnish humor (*Finnish humor channel*), quickly gained traction and the first short received nearly 600 views within a day. This unexpected success was encouraging and I continued to create content, bringing joy to others despite limited algorithmic support from YouTube.

Amid the struggles of my job search, a silver lining began to emerge. I noticed I had the time to improve skills I hadn't focused on before — video editing, coding and graphical design. I adopted healthier habits, exercised regularly and enjoyed more time in nature. I also dedicated time to writing and coding, which boosted both my skills and self-confidence. The lack of work-related stress allowed me to explore these interests deeply.

Reflecting on my unemployment, it's challenging to gauge how it compares to being employed because as we often do, we fantasize about the opposite situation. I had made a promise before leaving my last job to not continue if the conditions remained as stressful and devoid of hope for improvement. While I was relieved to leave that job, I also faced the paradox of not wanting to be unemployed.

As I write these final words, I'm still without a job after nearly five months of searching. Despite this, I remain hopeful and grateful that I am not facing financial strain. I am exploring alternative income sources and considering focusing solely on those opportunities if necessary. Until then, I will persist in my job search.

I wish you the best of luck in your own journey, regardless of your employment status. Keep striving and may you find success and fulfillment.

About the author

Joni Putkinen is a versatile author, YouTuber and front-end web developer with a passion for sports administration and governance. With a strong background in diverse fields and a drive to bridge the gap between his current skills and future aspirations, Joni approaches every project with enthusiasm and a keen eye for innovation.

Academic Background

Joni holds three master's degrees:

- Philosophy

- Sociology

- Social Sciences of Sport

These qualifications reflect his broad academic interests and deep commitment to understanding the world from multiple perspectives.

Joni's unique combination of skills and experiences informs his work and drives his creative projects. Despite facing unemployment several times, he remains optimistic and determined, always seeking new opportunities and challenges.

Thank you for reading my book!

Literature / suggested readings

About finding your own path:

Millerd, Paul. (2022). The *Pathless Path: Imagining a New Story for Work and Life.*

Pressfield, Steven. (2012). *Turning Pro.* Black Irish Entertainment.

Business:

Kaufman, Josh. (2010). *The Personal MBA: Master the Art of Business.* Portfolio / Penguin.

Sivers, Derek. (2015). *Anything You Want: 40 Lessons For a New Kind of Entrepreneur.* Portfolio / Penguin.

Sivers, Derek. (2020). *Hell Yeah or No: What's Worth Doing.* Hit Media.

Disappointments:

Kishimi, Ichiro & Koga, Fumitake. (2019). *The Courage To Be Disliked.* Allen Unwin.

Economics:

Sowell, Thomas. (2011). *Basic Economics: A Common Sense Guide to the Economy.* Basic Books, 4th Edition.

Habits:

Clear, James. (2018). *Atomic Habits.* Random House.

Money:

Housel, Morgan. (2020). *The Psychology of Money.* Harriman House.

Power & relationships:

Greene, Robert. (2000). *The 48 Laws of Power.* Penguin Books.

Greene, Robert. (2006). *The 33 Strategies of War.* Viking Books.

Probabilities, luck & risk:

Taleb, Nassim Nicholas. (2007). *Fooled By Randomness.* Penguin Books.

Taleb, Nassim Nicholas. (2010). *The Black Swan: The Impact of the Highly Improbable.* Random House.

Taleb, Nassim Nicholas. (2018). *Skin in the Game: Hidden Asymmetries in Daily Life.* Allen Lane.

Retirement:

Ferriss, Timothy. (2011). *4-Hour Work Week*. Ebury Press.

Self-confidence:

Schwartz, David. (2016). *The Magic of Thinking Big.* Random House.

Stoicism:

Aurelius, Marcus. (2002). *Meditations.* Translation by Gregory Hayes. Modern Library.

Seneca, Lucius Annaeus. (2023). *Letters from a Stoic. Seneca's Moral Letters to Lucilius.* Translation by Richard Mott Gummere. Classy Publishing.

www.ingramcontent.com/pod-product-compliance
Lightning Source LLC
Chambersburg PA
CBHW072152170526
45158CB00004BA/1614